Decorating Cakes
with
Chocolate

Decorating Cakes
with
Chocolate

Scrumptious Recipes and Original Chocolate Decorations

KATRIEN VAN ZYL

PHOTOGRAPHY BY JOHAN VAN ZYL

SEARCH PRESS

Star ratings:

1 ★ easy
2 ★★ in-between
3 ★★★ difficult

Note: Most of the projects are made using 10 cm (4 in.) high cake tiers. Each tier consists of 2 cake layers, each 5 cm (2 in.) high, stacked on top of each other. If the height of your cake tiers is less than 10 cm (4 in.), decrease the amount of choco-late for the decorations by up to half.

First published in Great Britain 2012
Search Press Limited
Wellwood, North Farm Road,
Tunbridge Wells, Kent, TN2 3DR

Originally published in South Africa in 2011 by Metz Press, 1 Cameronians Ave, Welgemoed 7530, South Africa

Copyright © Metz Press 2011
Copyright text © Katrien van Zyl
Photography copyright © Johan van Zyl

Publisher	Wilsia Metz
Photographer	Johan van Zyl
Design and layout	Liezl Maree
Proofreader	Amanda Taljaard
Reproduction	Robert Wong, Color/Fuzion
Print production	Andrew de Kock

Printed and bound in Singapore by Tien Wah Press

ISBN 978 1 84448 862 9

Contents

Introduction 7
Equipment list 8
Chocolate 12
Working with chocolate 14
Filling and coating cakes 19
Stacking cakes 21
Decorating a cake board 22

Basic recipes

Before you start baking 124
Serving guide 125
White chocolate mud cake 126
Dark chocolate mud cake 129
Chocolate chip cupcakes 132
Chocolate fruitcake 134
Chocolate carrot cake 137
Buttercream icing 140
Chocolate ganache filling 142
Chocolate ganache coating 144
Truffles 146
Chocolate paste 148

Chocolate projects

Diagonally striped ganache with dot flowers 24
Leaves and twigs 29
Gift box 34
Truffle tower 39
Small shavings and bows 42
Chocolate rose petal cake 47
Square spirals cake 52
Spiky cake 56
Pleated cake with filigree decorations 60
Shards and Christmas trees 64
Retro polka dot collar 69
Ice cream scoops 74
Triangles 77
Individual cakes 81
Polka panels 84
Candy-stripe curved collar 88
Funky rolls and shavings 93
Square polka dot cake 96
Cigarillos and truffles 99
Full lace collar 103
Light and dark stripes 106
Flaky shavings and lilies 110
Lace and collar 114
Wrinkled layered collar 118

Practical advice 150
Templates 157
Suppliers 159

Introduction

I do not know anyone who does not like chocolate in one form or another. One of my earliest memories is of my grandmother telling me: 'You're a chocoholic!' Although at the time I did not know what she meant, I have come to realize that she had foresight: I love chocolate and use it for creating decorations for cakes. Of all the cake decorating I have done, I most enjoy working with chocolate as it is such a versatile medium.

In this book I would like to show you how to work with chocolate to create beautifully decorated cakes. Whether you buy a ready-made cake or take the time to lovingly bake your own cake from the luscious recipes at the end of this book; whether you only bake occasionally or bake for profit, I would like to teach you a few techniques which, once mastered, will enable you to decorate your cake quickly and easily to be a show-stopper on any occasion.

This book features more than 20 chocolate-decorating projects from start to finish, as well as small chocolate decorations, mini cakes and cupcakes, showing you step by step how to create your own masterpieces. With a few handy tools and ordinary equipment, which can be bought at any grocery and hardware shop, anyone can make an exquisite cake.

As an added bonus, there are some tried and trusted cake and filling recipes at the end of the book, with guides for increasing the recipes to suit your needs, as well as templates to use in decorations.

Enjoy this chocolate experience!

Katrien

www.katrienscakes.co.za

Equipment list

The illustrated equipment is very useful to have at hand when you start making chocolate decorations:

Glass or Pyrex bowls

These bowls are preferable to plastic bowls as they retain heat better for the chocolate to stay pliable for longer. If you do not have glass or Pyrex, use microwave-safe plastic bowls for melting chocolate in the microwave oven or stainless steel bowls to heat chocolate over a simmering pot of water.

Metal or wooden spoons

Useful for stirring melted chocolate.

Scraper tool

Scrape melted chocolate onto your work surface to cool and thicken, then use to smooth chocolate onto the surface. Also use to scrape hardened chocolate off your work surface.

Plastic or metal scrapers

Used for evenly applying buttercream icing or ganache to the outside of cakes or for scraping melted chocolate onto your work surface. Plastic scrapers can be bought at baking supply shops and metal scrapers can be found at hardware shops.

Comb

Any plastic comb with wide-set teeth can be used to make grooves in slightly-set chocolate.

Silicone or plastic spatulas

Can be used instead of metal spoons. Silicone spatulas do not retain heat from the melted chocolate and cannot be bent out of shape by the heat.

Palette knife

An absolutely essential piece of equipment. Most of the projects ask for this tool as it is used to apply icing to your cake or to spread melted chocolate onto greaseproof paper.

Greaseproof paper

Also known as baking paper or parchment paper, it is used in making most of the projects in this book and can easily be found in supermarkets. It can be substituted with acetate paper or the type of plastic used for covering books (e.g. thin plastic or contact plastic with the paper backing left on), but greaseproof paper is the easiest and least expensive option.

Measuring tape

To measure the height, width and circumference of your cakes and your greaseproof paper templates.

Big and small knives

To make uneven chocolate rolls and to scrape hardened chocolate from your palette knife and scraper tools.

Pizza wheel

To cut chocolate panels easily by rolling over the chocolate with the pizza wheel.

Ice-cream scoop

To make chocolate rolls.

Melon baller

To make evenly sized round truffles.

Hand-held blender

Not essential but will help to smooth your tempered chocolate.

Hairdryer

Useful for slightly remelting chocolate which is setting too quickly, by blowing over it on a heated setting.

Cutters

Round, fluted or shaped cutters are used to make cut-out chocolate decorations.

Chopping board

Will make chopping your chocolate into small pieces much easier, but a food processor can also be used.

Ziploc plastic bags (resealable bags)

Sturdy plastic Ziploc bags are essential for storing chocolate and to use as piping bags. Make sure they are quite strong and will not tear at the sides. For small items even the plastic bank bags used for small change will do, as long as they are unused!

Cake boards

Sturdy board wrapped in foil, especially made to carry cakes, can be bought at baking supplies shops.

Plywood boards

Used as cake boards, can be cut to size at your hardware shop.

Glass plates

Used as cake boards, can be cut to size at your glass fitment shop. A thick, rectangular glass plate can also be used as a surface for making chocolate rolls.

Cake stands

Buy and collect different types of cakes stands from homeware shops.

Cardboard or foamalite plates

Can be used to separate cake layers. Cut your own boards from thick cardboard or foamalite to put in between cake tiers. Draw a template using your cake tin and cut it out with scissors. Cover the boards with plastic cling wrap to make them more hygienic.

Baking tins (sheets) or wooden trays

Used to transport your chocolate panels and decorations to your refrigerator and sometimes for shaping chocolate forms.

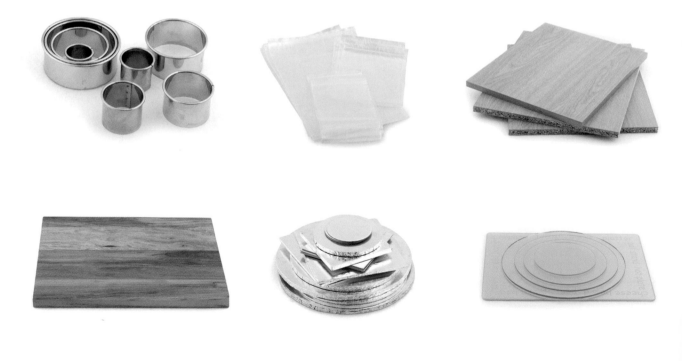

Marble or granite slab

Used as a surface for working your chocolate. Can be cut to size at a speciality shop or you can buy a marble cheeseboard from a homeware shop. The marble or granite helps the chocolate to cool and set more quickly, but a glass or ceramic tile will work as well.

Flat tile

A heavy tile with a smooth surface as well as a marble or granite slab can be used to work your chocolate as long as it does not slide when you are working on it. Place a piece of non-slip fabric underneath your tile to keep it in place and to protect your table.

Microwave oven

In my kitchen this is an essential piece of equipment which makes melting chocolate very easy, although chocolate can also be melted on the hob over a simmering pot of water or in an oven set at its lowest temperature.

Hot tray (warming tray)

Set at its lowest temperature, it will keep your melted chocolate pliable. I place a glass bowl on a folded dish towel on the hot tray so that the bowl is not in direct contact with the heat.

Laser or digital thermometer

Found at your hardware shop, this thermometer is very expensive but will make your life much easier as you can precisely monitor the temperature of your chocolate. By using my methods you should not have the problem of your chocolate spoiling but if you want to make extra sure, this thermometer can guide you. Make sure that you do not heat your chocolate above 45 °C (100 °F). I prefer to let chocolate cool down to 36 – 37 °C (97 – 99 °F) in winter and to 34 – 35 °C (93 – 95 °F) in summer to make my decorations.

Chocolate

Chocolate is made from the beans of the cacao tree. The ground beans are pressed to release the fat, or cocoa butter, leaving the cocoa mass or chocolate 'liquor'. The liquor, combined with the cocoa butter or other oils, is then used to make various kinds of chocolate. Some chocolate is best for eating and some for cooking, but either can be used for chocolate decorations.

Eating chocolate

Also known in the industry as 'couverture coating' or 'couverture chocolate'. Commercial names are, for example, 'Lindt 70% Dark', 'Cadbury Bournville' or 'Cadbury Dream', and 'Nestlé Milkybar', to name a few.

Cooking or baking chocolate

Also known as 'compound chocolate', 'coating chocolate', 'candy melts', 'candy coating' or 'confectionary coating'. Brand names are 'Orley Chocolate', 'Bakels Choccex', 'Chocolate Discs', 'Trumps Baking Chocolate Discs', 'Belgian Compound/Coating Chocolate' or 'Wilton's Candy Coating'.

What type of chocolate to use

We all love the smooth, rich taste of 'eating', 'Swiss' or 'Belgian' chocolate bars. However, for decorating purposes, this type of chocolate is not very stable, as it has a high fat content and does not set easily. It can be used with great success if you apply lots of patience and use the tempering method in preparation. Eating chocolate takes much longer to set, but you can use this to your advantage, especially when making chocolate collars, as you have a longer window in which to attach the chocolate to the cake.

When making decorations with eating chocolate only, it can take up to half an hour or longer to set. If you want the chocolate to set more quickly you can place a baking tin (sheet) in the refrigerator for 20 minutes, to have a cool surface to work on, and then proceed to make your decorations on the cold sheet. If you find that your chocolate has not set after 45 minutes, you have probably overheated it or the room temperature is too high. You can try to rectify this problem by remelting and retempering the chocolate, as explained later, or by placing your decorations in the refrigerator for a few minutes to set slightly.

Cooking (baking) chocolate has a much lower cocoa butter content than other chocolate varieties. It is relatively stable, can withstand fairly high heat and is easier to use for making decorations, because it sets more quickly than eating chocolate and therefore you have to make your decorations quickly. You will have to experiment with different varieties of chocolate to find out what works best for you.

One thing you should avoid though, is using chocolate chips when the recipe calls for melting the chocolate. The low cocoa butter content makes chips perfect for remaining whole at high heat, such as in chocolate chip cookies and muffins, but unsuitable for melting and moulding.

I prefer to use a combination of cooking and eating chocolate, using ⅔ cooking chocolate to ⅓ of eating chocolate in most of my decorations.

Tip

If you are hesitant about the process of colouring chocolate, remember that the contrasting shades of white chocolate, milk chocolate, caramel chocolate and dark chocolate can also be very effective in decorations.

Working with chocolate

The three important steps when working with chocolate are melting, tempering and colouring.

Melting

Be very cautious when heating chocolate so that it does not overheat or burn. Chocolate scorches and spoils easily, becoming lumpy and grainy. Melting chocolate requires a very gentle heat and lots of patience!

I recommend using a microwave oven because it is easy and fast, but you can also melt the chocolate in a bowl over a lightly simmering pot of water (but do take care that none of the condensed steam drips into the bowl or the chocolate will clump up or seize and become unworkable). The chocolate can also be melted in an oven set at its lowest temperature, or on a hot (warming) tray.

Tempering

This step is the secret to a professional finish for your chocolate decorations, especially if you are working with eating or couverture chocolate. Tempered chocolate is stable enough to be moulded and worked into a variety of shapes and can keep for months at cool room temperature.

The process is not complicated, as all it involves is to quickly lower the temperature of the melted chocolate and to agitate it. This helps to form the crystal structure which makes chocolate harden with a smooth, shiny finish and causes that satisfying snap when a piece is broken off. If the melted chocolate is allowed to cool on its own without tempering, it will appear dull, remain soft and feel greasy to the touch as the cocoa butter rises to the surface, making unsightly white streaks as it sets.

I use a quick-tempering method that almost guarantees a perfect end product.

Recommended melting method 1

If you are using cooking chocolate only, or a mix of ⅔ cooking chocolate to ⅓ eating chocolate, this is the recommended method.

1. Chop the chocolate into evenly sized pieces for even melting and place in a glass bowl (glass keeps the heat of the chocolate longer than plastic does).

2. Melt the pieces in a microwave oven at 20% power or on the defrost setting and stir at 1 to 2-minute intervals.

3. Finish heating when most, but not all, of the chocolate is melted. There must still be a few visible chunks. Remove from the microwave oven and stir continuously until it is smooth, shiny, and completely melted.

4. Because cooking chocolate is so stable, it is not necessary to temper it further.

If you have inadvertently melted the chocolate fully, with no unmelted chunks visible, your chocolate will be too hot to work with. Rectify this by adding 1 tablespoon or up to ¼ of the original weight of chopped chocolate to the fully-melted chocolate and stir continuously until it is smooth and completely melted. This will lower the temperature of the chocolate slightly, making it easier to work with and is similar to the quick-tempering method explained below.

Recommended melting and tempering method 2

This is the recommended method if you are using a larger percentage of eating chocolate to cooking chocolate, working with more than 450 g (1 lb) of eating chocolate or working with couverture chocolate.

1. Chop all the required chocolate into evenly sized pieces for even melting and place ⅔ of the chocolate in a glass bowl. Keep the rest of the chopped pieces at hand.

2. Melt the pieces in a microwave oven at 20% power or on the defrost setting and stir at 1 to 2-minute intervals.

3. Finish heating when most, but not all, of the chocolate is melted. There must still be a few visible chunks. Remove from the microwave oven and stir continuously until it is smooth, shiny, and completely melted.

4. Add the remaining ⅓ of the chocolate pieces and stir this into the already fully melted chocolate. The warm chocolate will melt the chopped chocolate, and the newly added chocolate will bring down the temperature of the warm chocolate.

5. Stir very well until all the chocolate is melted, or alternatively use a hand-held electric blender until the chocolate is melted and smooth. If you see a few lumps remaining in the melted chocolate after stirring or blending for a while, put it back in the microwave oven and heat gently at 20% power or on the defrost setting, stirring at 20-second intervals. Or place it back over a pot of simmering water or in the oven at the lowest temperature or on a hot tray until it is completely melted.

Colouring chocolate

Food colouring is available in many forms, such as liquid, powder or paste (gel). In some countries an oil-based colouring specifically for chocolate is available, but this can be difficult to find. However, I have had great success in colouring chocolate without having to use special colouring.

Liquid food colouring

This can be bought at any supermarket and is usually available in pink, red, blue, yellow and green. Because liquid food colouring is water-based, it can affect the texture of the chocolate or thicken it so that it becomes unusable. If you use this, be sure to follow my method of mixing it with vegetable oil and then heating. Use an eye-dropper, which you can buy at your pharmacy, for precisely measuring out the drops of liquid food colouring.

Powder food colouring

This can be bought at baking supply shops and is available in many colours. Powder food colouring is also mixed with vegetable oil as it can clump together when mixed with chocolate, causing your chocolate to become grainy or streaked with colour particles.

Paste (gel) food colouring

This can be bought at baking supply shops and is available in many colours. It is the easiest colouring to work with as it doesn't affect the chocolate too much and can be added directly to your chocolate.

Recommended colouring method

Remember that white chocolate, coloured with powder or paste food colouring, is best for bright colours. Start by using 100 g (3½ oz) of white chocolate and follow the directions for standard amounts of colouring precisely. Add the colouring to the chocolate after it has been melted as described on p. 15. If you want to colour the chocolate a darker shade, keep on adding colouring and vegetable oil in the ratio given in the recommended colouring method, but do not exceed these amounts: too much colouring and the chocolate will become brittle and have a bitter aftertaste; too much oil and the chocolate will become too soft to work with.

1. Melt 100 g (3½ oz) of white chocolate as per the method on p. 15.

2. **If using liquid food colouring**: Mix 2 – 10 drops of liquid food colouring with 1.25 – 2.5 ml (¼ – ½ tsp) vegetable oil and heat in a microwave oven at full power for 5 seconds to warm slightly. Do not exceed 15 drops (¼ tsp) of liquid food colouring or 5 ml (1 tsp) of oil. Stir the mixture into the melted chocolate.

3. **If using powder food colouring**: Mix 1.6 – 1.25 ml (⅛-¼ tsp) of the coloured powder with 1.25 – 2.5 ml (¼-½ tsp) vegetable oil and stir the mixture into the melted chocolate. Do not exceed 2.5 ml (½ tsp) coloured powder or 5 ml (1 tsp) oil.

4. **If using paste (gel) food colouring**: Put a few drops at a time directly into the melted chocolate and stir until fully incorporated. Do not exceed 5 drops of paste food colouring.

5. Spoon the coloured chocolate into a Ziploc bag and use to make decorations or use the coloured chocolate as per the project instructions.

Adding liquids to chocolate

Sometimes a recipe calls for liquids like milk, cream, flavouring or liqueur to be added to melted chocolate, for instance in ganache filling. Never add cold liquids to melted chocolate, as that can cause the chocolate to seize. Instead, ensure that your liquids are warm when you add them or alternatively heat the chocolate and the liquid together in the same bowl, gently whisking until the liquid has been completely incorporated.

Problems and watch points

- If by any chance you have overheated your chocolate and it has lost its shine and become grainy, immediately pour it into a cool bowl, add chunks of solid chocolate, and stir continuously. You might save your whole batch that way.
- If you have inadvertently heated the chocolate in the microwave oven until fully, instead of partly melted you can still save it by using the quick-tempering method. Add 15 ml (1 tbsp) or up to ¼ of the original weight of chopped chocolate into the fully melted chocolate and stir continuously until it is smooth and completely melted.
- If your melted chocolate seizes because it has come into contact with liquid, the only way to save the chocolate is to add more water, cream or milk until the mixture becomes a syrup. Unfortunately, this chocolate syrup cannot be used as pure chocolate for decorative purposes any longer, but can be used in a variety of other recipes.
- If after adding liquid colouring the chocolate thickens too much, either add another 2.5 ml (½ tsp) of oil (never exceeding 5 ml (1 tsp) altogether) and stir, or add 15 ml (1 tbsp) of chopped solid chocolate, put the bowl back in the microwave oven and heat at 20% power or on the defrost setting, stirring at 20-second intervals until the chocolate is spreadable. Note that you can still spread the chocolate even if it is not runny.
- When spreading melted chocolate on your work surface, you might experience that the surface of the chocolate sets more quickly than the chocolate at the bottom. The hardened chocolate will crumble as you're spreading. This could happen for various reasons: Was the chocolate overheated? Was the chocolate fully melted instead of partly melted before tempering? Are you using the correct method of spreading and scraping the chocolate on your work surface until slightly thickened or did you pour it out and spread it flat immediately? Wait for the chocolate to set and remelt the chocolate in the microwave oven, making sure to stop when there are still a few unmelted chunks visible and then stirring continuously until it is smooth, shiny and completely melted.
- It is very difficult to work with chocolate in extreme room temperatures, e.g. below 10 °C (50 °F) or above 30 °C (86 °F), as the chocolate will either set too quickly and crack, set too slowly or not at all. It might be necessary for you to heat your work surface with heated towels or an electric blanket or to cool it down by placing a piece of plastic over the surface and putting ice on top of the plastic. If you are working with a loose marble slab, flat tile or rectangular glass plate you can either place it in a lukewarm oven or in the refrigerator for a short while.
- If you find tiny holes in your chocolate panels or chocolate collar after the paper template has been removed, it means that too much air was incorporated into your melted chocolate while you were stirring it and the air bubbles burst when the chocolate was spread on the paper. Prevent this by tapping your bowl of chocolate on a folded dish towel on your work surface for the air bubbles to rise to the surface and break before you start using it. You can fill any holes with some melted chocolate poured into a Ziploc bag and piped directly into the hole.

Filling and coating cakes

It is important to cover your cake with a coating of ganache or buttercream icing for the chocolate decorations to adhere to when you put them on the cake. If you are using a shop-bought cake, make sure that it is iced all over or otherwise make up a batch of ganache or buttercream icing from the recipes on p. 140 and p. 144 and spread it all over the cake.

I prefer to bake the cake the day before so that it can firm up. The baked cakes can be left in their tins overnight and then divided, filled and coated the next day.

Be sure to look at the sections on stacking cakes and decorating a cake board before you proceed to fill your cake.

Note: Any round or square cake is usually baked in two baking tins, yielding two layers each about 5 cm (2 in.) high. Each layer can be sliced and filled with buttercream, yielding four layers, which, stuck on top of each other, forms a whole cake approximately 10 cm (4 in.) high. When stacked with other cakes, it becomes a tier in a many-tiered cake.

Filling and coating

1. Neaten each cake by cutting off the crunchy top part. Each cake can also be divided into two layers by cutting it in half horizontally using the following method:
   - Measure the height of the sides of the cake, divide by 2 and at the correct height, stick toothpicks into four sides of the cake so that they stick out horizontally as a guide.
   - Take a long piece of sewing thread or nylon fishing line or dental floss (not the peppermint flavoured kind!) and place it around the cake, lightly resting on top of the toothpicks.
   - Pull the ends of the thread towards and across each other so that it cuts into the cake. Pull until the thread is free and you have two neatly divided layers.

2. Place one layer on your cake board, serving plate or cake stand. For a single-tiered cake or the bottom tier of a multi-tiered cake, the board or serving plate should be 10 cm (4 in.) wider than the cake. If the cake will be used as part of the tiers, the board should be the same size as the cake.

3. If you want your filling to be even you can pipe it on by pouring the filling into a big Ziploc bag and snipping off one corner to make a big piping bag. Start in the centre and circle the ganache filling or buttercream icing towards the outside edge. Otherwise dollop a few spoonfuls of filling onto the cake layer and spread it with your palette knife or spatula.

4. Place another layer of cake on top of the first and repeat the filling process. Layer and fill until the whole cake has been stacked.

5. The filled cake can be frozen for use at a later date or left in the refrigerator overnight. This will give you a firmer cake to decorate, but let the cake reach room temperature before coating. If you are pressed for time, coat the cake directly after filling.

6. Coat the cake with ganache coating or buttercream icing by spreading it on with your palette knife or spatula or place the coating into a big Ziploc bag and pipe it onto the cake. Smooth the piped coating with your palette knife or a spatula.

Note: If you have frozen your filled cake beforehand be sure to defrost it thoroughly and let it reach room temperature before decorating.

Stacking cakes

Two, three and four-tier cakes are stacked on top of each other with each tier on its own board. The boards can be shop-bought cake boards, chipboard, plywood boards, thick foamalite or thick cardboard cut to the size of each cake tier and covered with plastic cling wrap.

Wooden dowelling sticks, wooden skewers, straws or hollow PVC pipes are inserted into the tiers to hold the weight of the cakes placed on top of each other.

1. Before placing a layer of cake on the cake board, put a dollop of ganache or icing on the board to act like glue, holding the cake in place. Fill and cover each cake directly on a board (or put your shop-bought cake on a board).

2. Push 3 – 6 wooden sticks randomly into the bottom tier, the biggest cake, and mark the sticks with a pen at the level of the top of the cake. Now pull the sticks out slightly, trim them at the mark with scissors or shears and push them back down into the cake. They will take the weight of the tiers that follow so that your cake does not collapse.

3. Spread some ganache or buttercream icing over the top of the cake where the sticks are inserted.

4. Now proceed with filling the rest of the layers. Gently lift the next tier with your hand and an egg lifter and place it in the centre of the bottom cake.

5. Adjust the placed cake to sit centrally over the bottom cake. If you want to be very accurate, use a ruler and measure the rim of the bottom cake that juts out. Slide the placed cake until the amount of cake showing is even all round.

6. Place the next smaller sized cake centrally over the middle tier, judging the position by eye or measuring it with a ruler.

7. If you find that the cakes are very heavy when making a 3 or 4-tiered cake, reinforce the cake by also putting sticks into the middle tiers.

8. If, after stacking the tiers, some of the in-between cake boards show, pipe a thin line of ganache coating or buttercream icing onto the board, around the cake.

Decorating a cake board

Items needed

- ✓ A cake board or a plywood board cut to size, as per the project instructions
- ✓ 150 g (5½ oz) melted chocolate (use any leftover melted chocolate or remelt any hardened bits of chocolate from your project)
- ✓ Ribbon as wide as the rim and as long as the circumference of the board
- ✓ Double-sided adhesive tape or non-toxic glue (e.g. Pritt)

Method

1. Pour the melted chocolate onto the cake board or plywood board.
2. Use a palette knife to smooth out the chocolate.
3. Leave the chocolate to set or sprinkle some chocolate shavings onto the chocolate before it sets.
4. With a sharp knife neaten the edges of the board by cutting off any chocolate that has spilled over the edges.
5. Coat the edges with non-toxic glue or put double-sided adhesive tape around the board.
6. Attach the ribbon to the glue around the board.
7. Glue the ends of the ribbon where they overlap.

Chocolate projects

Diagonally striped ganache with dot flowers

For a thoughtful memento of the party, decorate some cupcakes in the same way to present to each guest to take home.

This cake has lots of colourful flowers for a girl's birthday party or even for a christening. Makes up to 50 servings.

Chocolate dot flowers ★

At the back of this book are templates for flowers (see p. 157). Copy the design a few times on paper that will fit into a baking tin (sheet) or wooden tray.

- Each 100 g (3½ oz) of melted chocolate will make about 12 flowers.
- The following recipe is for up to 80 flowers, using 600 g (1¼ lb) white chocolate coloured by following the instructions on p. 17: 'Colouring chocolate'. Pour each of the colours into a separate Ziploc bag which you will use as a piping bag.

To colour the chocolate

1. Yellow chocolate: 100 g (3½ oz) white chocolate, melted and coloured with 2.5 ml (½ tsp) cooking vegetable oil mixed with 10 drops of yellow liquid food colouring or 2 or more drops of paste food colouring.

2. Orange chocolate: 100 g (3½ oz) white chocolate, melted and coloured with 2.5 ml (½ tsp) cooking vegetable oil mixed with 2 drops of red and 8 drops of yellow liquid food colouring (to make orange) or 2 or more drops of paste food colouring.

3. Red chocolate: 100 g (3½ oz) white chocolate, melted and coloured with 2.5 ml (½ tsp) vegetable oil mixed with 10 drops of red liquid food colouring or 2 or more drops of paste food colouring.

4. Blue chocolate: 100 g (3½ oz) white chocolate, melted and coloured with 2.5 ml (½ tsp) vegetable oil mixed with 10 drops of blue liquid food colouring or 2 or more drops of paste food colouring.

5. Purple chocolate: 100 g (3½ oz) white chocolate, melted and coloured with 2.5 ml (½ tsp) vegetable oil mixed with 8 drops of blue and 2 drops of red liquid food colouring (to make purple) or 2 or more drops of paste food colouring.

6. Green chocolate: 100 g (3½ oz) white chocolate, melted and coloured with 2.5 ml (½ tsp) vegetable oil mixed with 10 drops of green liquid food colouring or 2 or more drops of paste food colouring.

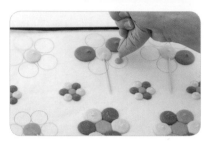

To create the flowers

1. Assemble all your equipment.
2. Copy the flower template on p. 157 several times on paper and place these on a baking tin (sheet) or wooden tray that will fit into your refrigerator. It will help if you prepare more than one tray as you will need to repeat the process several times.
3. Cut see-through greaseproof paper to line the tray prepared with your flower template, place it over the template and secure the paper by sticking it to the tray with adhesive tape or masking tape. If working with eating chocolate only, you can put the tray in the refrigerator for 20 minutes before making your decorations on it.
4. Snip off a small piece at one corner of each individual Ziploc bag of coloured chocolate to make piping bags.
5. Following the design on your template, pipe big centre dots of yellow and green, or of a different colour, onto the paper.
6. Pipe dots of the same or different colours around each centre to form a flower.
7. If you want some of the dot flowers to stand upright in your cake, place toothpicks in some of the big centre dots when you start so that the chocolate sets over one point of the toothpick.
8. When your tray is full, place the tray containing dot flowers in the refrigerator for no longer than 10 minutes for the chocolate to set and harden.
9. Take the tray out of the refrigerator and pull the flowers off the paper.
10. Repeat the steps until all the chocolate has been used.

Make the complete cake ★★

- ✓ 3 round cakes (each 2 layers) of decreasing sizes: 20 cm (8 in.),15 cm (6 in.) and 10 cm (4 in.) in diameter
- ✓ 1 round 30 cm (12 in.) cake board, plywood board or cake stand
- ✓ 1 round 15 cm (6 in.) divider made from thick cardboard or foamalite, wrapped in aluminium foil or plastic cling wrap
- ✓ 1 round 10 cm (4 in.) divider made from thick cardboard or foamalite, wrapped in aluminium foil or plastic cling wrap
- ✓ 2 batches each of chocolate ganache filling and coating of your choice (recipes p. 142 and p. 144)
- ✓ A cheap steel fork with the two middle prongs removed with a steel cutter
- ✓ Chocolate dot flowers made with:
    - 600 g (1¼ lb) white chocolate
    - 15 ml (1 tbsp) vegetable oil
    - Food colouring such as yellow, red, blue and green
- ✓ 100 g (3½ oz) dark or milk chocolate melted, to attach the flowers

Note: The three-tiered cake in this project is about 30 cm (12 in.) high. If your cake is smaller, decrease the amounts of ganache and chocolate needed.

Assembling the cake

For a three-tiered cake as illustrated, you will need 3 ready-made round layer cakes of decreasing sizes. Use any of the recipes at the back of this book to bake delicious cakes in three different sizes.

You will also need three cake boards. For the bottom layer, use a round cake board, plywood board or cake stand which is slightly larger in diameter than the cake, namely 30 cm (12 in.). For the middle and top layers, use a cake board, foamalite plate or a piece of cardboard covered in plastic cling wrap with the same diameter as the cake so that it will not show on the finished cake.

1. Make a double batch of ganache coating (p. 144) with dark or milk chocolate.
2. Divide each layer horizontally (see instructions on p. 19: 'Filling and coating cakes'), fill with the ganache filling, stack each cake, and then coat each cake with ganache.
3. Stack the tiers according to the instructions on p. 21: 'Stacking cakes'.

Note: Any round cake is usually baked in two baking tins, yielding two layers; each about 5 cm (2 in.) high. Each layer can be sliced and filled with buttercream, yielding four layers, which, stuck on top of each other, form a whole cake. This becomes a tier of 10 cm (4 in.) or more when stacked with other cakes in a many-tiered cake.

Decorating the cake

1. If the leftover ganache coating has set, remelt it in the microwave oven at 20% power or on the defrost setting, stirring at 1-minute intervals until the ganache is runny and spreadable.

2. Spread a thin layer of ganache over all the stacked cake tiers and smooth it out with the palette knife.

3. Use the modified fork to draw a diagonal pattern in the ganache from the bottom of each cake layer to the top until the whole cake has a diagonal pattern.

4. Pour the 100 g (3½ oz) melted chocolate into a Ziploc bag and snip off a corner to make a piping bag. Pipe some chocolate onto the back of each dot flower before you press it onto the cake. The setting chocolate will act as glue, attaching the flowers to the cake.

5. Press the ends of the toothpicks holding flowers into the cake to raise it to a new dimension.

6. If you have not used a cake stand or serving plate, follow the method on p. 22: 'Decorating a cake board'.

Cupcakes

1. Spread ganache coating over the tops of your cupcakes until the coating is smooth.

2. Wait for it to set slightly and then scrape a diagonal pattern into the ganache with your modified fork.

3. Press a dot flower onto the ganache.

Leaves and twigs

Any gardener will love this cake. Make the leaves in white and green chocolate for a spring-fresh look or create an autumn look with orange, yellow and red leaves.

Makes up to 40 servings.

Chocolate leaves ★

Pick an assortment of leaves in your garden or use only one type. Leave the stems on where possible. Suitable leaves are ivy, rose, cabbage, mint, lemon or vine leaves. Ensure that the plants are non-toxic and that the leaves have not been sprayed with insecticide. Wash and dry them thoroughly.

- Each 100 g (3½ oz) of chocolate will make up to 20 leaves.
- This project is for 100 chocolate leaves made with 500 g (1 lb 2 oz) of chocolate.

To prepare the chocolate

Depending on the colour scheme you select, melt and colour the chocolate by following the instructions on p. 15: 'Recommended melting method 1 or 2' and p. 17: 'Colouring chocolate', for instance:

1. Dark chocolate: 100 g (3½ oz), melted
2. Caramel chocolate: 100 g (3½ oz), melted
3. Orange chocolate: 100 g (3½ oz) white chocolate, melted and coloured with 2.5 ml (½ tsp) vegetable oil mixed with 2 drops of red and 8 drops of yellow liquid food colouring (to make orange) or 2 or more drops of paste food colouring.
4. Lime green chocolate: 100 g (3½ oz) white chocolate, melted and coloured with 2.5 ml (½ tsp) vegetable oil mixed with 2 drops of green and 8 drops of yellow liquid food colouring (to make lime green) or 2 or more drops of paste food colouring.
5. Dark green chocolate: 100 g (3½ oz) white chocolate, melted and coloured with 2.5 ml (½ tsp) vegetable oil mixed with 2 drops of green and 8 drops of blue liquid food colouring (to make dark green) or 2 or more drops of paste food colouring.

Tips
- The leaves and twigs can be made up to two weeks ahead and stored in an airtight container in a cool, dark cupboard.
- Instead of twigs you could use dark chocolate rolls or cigarillos (p. 99).
- Any leftover leaves and twigs can be remelted and used for other decorations.

To create the leaves

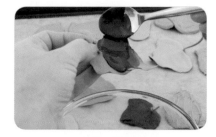

1. Cut a piece of greaseproof paper to line a baking tin (sheet) or wooden tray that will fit into your refrigerator. (As you will need to repeat this several times, it will help if you prepare more than one tray.)

2. Secure the paper by sticking it to the tray with adhesive tape or masking tape.

3. Take a leaf in one hand or hold it by the stem. Using a teaspoon, place a dollop of melted chocolate on the back of the leaf, where the veins are more prominent, and spread the chocolate all over this side.

4. Carefully place the leaf with the chocolate side up on the greaseproof paper and leave to set slightly.

5. If the coating looks too thin and fragile, spread another layer of chocolate over the first layer.

6. If the chocolate in the bowl starts to set while you are making your leaves, reheat the chocolate by placing the bowl in the microwave oven at 20% power or on the defrost setting, stirring at 20-second intervals.

7. Repeat with the other leaves, using the different colours you chose. You could also mix two different colours on a leaf to give a marbled effect.

8. When your tray is full or all the leaves are coated, place the tray with leaves in the refrigerator for no longer than 10 minutes for the chocolate to set and harden.

9. Take the tray out of the refrigerator and peel the chocolate leaves off the real leaves by holding the leaves by their stems.

Chocolate twigs

1. Prepare a baking tin (sheet) or wooden tray with greaseproof paper as above, securing the paper to the tray. If working with eating chocolate, you can place the tray in the refrigerator for 20 minutes before making your twigs on it, to help the chocolate set.

2. Melt 100 g (3½ oz) dark chocolate in the microwave oven by following the instructions on p. 15: 'Recommended melting method 1 or 2'. Pour it into a small Ziploc bag and snip off a corner to make a piping bag.

3. Pipe the dark chocolate free-hand onto the paper to make twigs. Let them set slightly and repipe over all the twigs so that they are thick and strong.

4. When your tray is full or all the chocolate has been used, place the tray with twigs in the refrigerator for no longer than 10 minutes for the chocolate to set and harden.

5. Take the tray out of the refrigerator and peel the twigs off the paper.

Make the complete cake ★★

✓ 2 round cakes (each 2 layers) of 20 cm (8 in.) and 15 cm (6 in.)
✓ 1 round 25 cm (10 in.) cake board, plywood board or cake stand
✓ 1 round 10 cm (4 in.) divider made from thick cardboard or foamalite, wrapped in aluminium foil or plastic cling wrap
✓ 1½ batch of plain buttercream icing (recipe p. 140) or 1½ batch each of white chocolate ganache filling and coating (recipes p. 142 and p. 144)
✓ 100 chocolate leaves made with:
  100 g (3½ oz) dark chocolate
  100 g (3½ oz) caramel chocolate
  300 g (10½ oz) white chocolate
  7.5 ml (1½ tsp) vegetable oil
  Food colouring such as yellow, red, green and blue
✓ Chocolate twigs made with 100 g (3½ oz) dark chocolate
✓ 200 g (7 oz) white chocolate to attach the leaves

Note: This two-tiered cake is about 20 cm (8 in.) high. If your cake is smaller, decrease the amounts of buttercream, ganache and chocolate needed.

Assembling the cake

For the cake resembling plant pots, as illustrated, you will need two ready-made round cakes of different sizes, namely 20 cm (8 in.) and 15 cm (6 in.) in diameter. Use any of the recipes at the back of this book to create two cakes in your favourite flavour.

You will also need two cake boards. For the bottom layer, use a round cake board, plywood board or cake stand which is only slightly larger in diameter than the cake, namely 25 cm (10 in.). For the top layer, use a cake board, foamalite plate or a piece of cardboard covered in plastic cling wrap which is smaller in diameter than the cake, namely 10 cm (4 in.). This is because you are going to carve away around the bottom of the cakes to shape flowerpots.

1. Divide each layer horizontally (see instructions on p. 19: 'Filling and coating cakes'), fill with buttercream icing or chocolate ganache filling and stack each cake. Do not coat the cakes at this stage.

2. After filling, refrigerate or freeze your cakes for an hour to make it easier to cut them.

3. Cut two round pieces of paper to use as templates for cutting out the flowerpots, one of 15 cm (6 in.) and the other 10 cm (4 in.) in diameter.

4. Place the larger filled cake on a cutting board, placing the larger template in the centre of the cake and stick a toothpick into the paper to keep it in place.

5. Cut the cake at an angle from the paper to the bottom of the cake, slanting the sides and shaping it into a flowerpot.

6. Repeat with the smaller cake, using the smaller template as a guide.

7. Remove the paper and turn the cakes upside down, with the widest parts on top. Place each on its own cake board.

8. Coat each tier with the rest of the buttercream or ganache and stack by following the method on p. 21.

Tip

Use the cut-off pieces of cake to make cake crumbs in a food processor. Mix equal weights of cake crumbs and melted chocolate. Scoop out with a teaspoon and form into balls to make delicious cake truffles. Leave them to set in a refrigerator. Use as is, or coat with melted chocolate.

Decorating the cake

1. Pour the 200 g (7 oz) melted white chocolate into a Ziploc bag and snip off a corner to make a piping bag.

2. Cover the cake with chocolate leaves by piping melted chocolate onto the back of each leaf and pressing it onto the cake.

3. Work from the top of the cake downwards, layering the leaves over each other until you reach the bottom of the cake.

4. If the chocolate in the Ziploc bag starts to set while you are attaching the leaves, reheat the whole bag in the microwave oven at 20% power or on the defrost setting for 20-second intervals.

5. Push the twigs randomly into the tops of each cake tier.

6. If you have not used a cake stand or serving plate, follow the method on p. 22: 'Decorating a cake board'.

Mini cakes ★

Cupcakes are already shaped like little flowerpots, inviting you to decorate them with chocolate flowers or leaves.

1. Remove the paper wrappers from your cupcakes and stick two cupcakes together with plain buttercream icing or white chocolate ganache filling.

2. Coat your mini cakes with the buttercream or ganache.

3. Dab melted chocolate on the backs of chocolate leaves and press onto the cakes.

4. Add a few twigs to the tops of the mini cakes.

Gift box

Give a lovely chocolate cake gift box decorated with chocolate hearts and topped with chocolate-dipped berries. It is sure to be a heartfelt gift for anyone, especially on Valentine's Day.

Makes up to 30 servings.

Chocolate piped hearts ★

At the back of this book are templates for hearts (see p. 157). Copy the design a few times on paper that will fit into a baking tin (sheet) or wooden tray. 100 g (3½ oz) of chocolate will make up to 20 hearts.

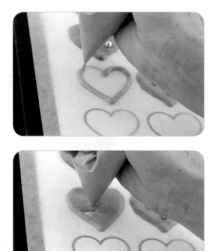

To prepare the chocolate

1. Make red or pink hearts by melting 100 g (3½ oz) white chocolate according to the instructions on p. 15: 'Recommended melting method 1 or 2'.
2. Colour the melted chocolate with 2.5 ml (½ tsp) vegetable oil mixed with 2 drops of red or pink food colouring according to the instructions on p. 17: 'Colouring chocolate'.
3. Pour the coloured chocolate into a Ziploc bag and snip off one corner to make a piping bag.

To create the hearts

1. Cut a piece of see-through greaseproof paper to line the tray prepared with your heart template and secure the paper by sticking it to the tray with adhesive tape or masking tape. If working with eating chocolate only, you can put the tray in the refrigerator for 20 minutes before making your decorations on it.
2. Following the design on your template, pipe an outline of a heart onto the paper with the coloured melted chocolate.
3. Fill in the rest of the heart with the chocolate.
4. While the chocolate is still runny, place some silver dragees or candy beads onto the hearts.
5. Continue piping and filling hearts. If the chocolate in the Ziploc bag starts to set, heat the bag in the microwave oven at 50% power for 10 seconds.
6. When your tray is full, place the tray with hearts in the refrigerator for no longer than 10 minutes for the chocolate to set and harden.
7. Take the tray out of the refrigerator and peel the hearts from the paper.

Chocolate-dipped strawberries ★

✓ Punnet of strawberries (±25)
✓ 100 g (3½ oz) white chocolate, melted according to the instructions on p. 15: 'Recommended melting method 1 or 2'

1. Wash and dry the strawberries, keeping the stems on.
2. Cut a piece of greaseproof paper to line a baking tin (sheet) or wooden tray that will fit into your refrigerator.
3. Keeping hold of the stems, dip the ends of the strawberries into the melted chocolate and place them on the tray.
4. When all the strawberries have been dipped, place the tray in the refrigerator. When required, peel the strawberries off the paper.

Tip

Prepare the chocolate-dipped strawberries only a few hours before you need them and keep them in the refrigerator as they last for only up to one day. Decorate your cake with the strawberries just prior to serving.

Chocolate-dipped, heart-decorated biscuits

1. Cut a piece of greaseproof paper to line a baking tin (sheet) or wooden tray that will fit into your refrigerator.
2. Melt 225 g (½ lb) milk chocolate.
3. Dip each wafer biscuit into the melted milk chocolate and place it on the tray, chocolate side up.
4. When all the biscuits have been dipped or the tray is full, place in the refrigerator for no longer than 10 minutes for the chocolate to set.
5. Melt 50 g (2 oz) white chocolate and colour it with 1.25 ml (¼ tsp) vegetable oil mixed with 1 drop of red or pink food colouring.
6. Pour the coloured chocolate into a Ziploc bag and snip off one corner to make a piping bag.
7. Pipe free-hand hearts onto some or all of the biscuits on the tray by squeezing the piping bag to make a 'cone' shape first on one and then on the other side for a full heart.
8. Place a silver dragee in the centre of the piped heart.
9. Place the tray in the refrigerator again for no longer than 5 minutes.

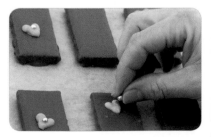

Make the complete cake ★

- ✓ 1 rectangular sheet cake of 23 x 30 cm (9 x 12 in.), 5 cm (2 in.) high
- ✓ 1 rectangular cake board, plywood board or cake stand
- ✓ ½ batch of chocolate buttercream icing (recipe p. 141) or ½ batch each of dark chocolate ganache filling and coating (recipes p. 142 and p. 144)
- ✓ 2 packets of wafer biscuits or any rectangular biscuits
- ✓ 225 g (½ lb) milk chocolate for dipping
- ✓ Red or pink chocolate for piping made with:
     - 50 g (2 oz) white chocolate
     - 1.25 ml (¼ tsp) vegetable oil
     - 1 drop of red or pink food colouring
- ✓ 20 chocolate hearts made with:
     - 100 g (3½ oz) white chocolate
     - 2.5 ml (½ tsp) vegetable oil
     - Red or pink food colouring
     - Silver dragees (candy beads)
- ✓ 25 chocolate-dipped strawberries made with:
     - 1 punnet of strawberries
     - 100 g (3½ oz) white chocolate

Assembling the cake

To make the gift box, the sides of the cake are covered with chocolate-dipped and heart-decorated biscuits protruding over the top of the cake to create a space you can fill to the brim with chocolate hearts and chocolate-dipped strawberries.

1. Cut the rectangular cake in half. Save one half to use for making mini cakes or freeze for use at a later time.

2. Slice the remaining half horizontally into two layers, using toothpicks and string as explained on p. 19. Fill with your choice of chocolate buttercream icing or dark chocolate ganache filling, stacking one layer on top of the other.

3. Place on a cake board and coat the whole cake with the rest of the buttercream or ganache coating.

4. To work out how many biscuits you will need to cover the sides of the cake completely, you will have to do some calculations:
   - Measure the width of each of the 4 sides of the cake and find the total.
   - Measure the width of a biscuit and divide this into the total width of the cake.
   - This gives you the number of biscuits needed to encircle the cake in one layer.

Note: Ideally you want the biscuits to hide the cake completely, without any gaps. You might have to trim off a sliver from the sides of your cake for the biscuits to fit perfectly.

Decorating the cake

1. To attach the biscuits to the cake, use any leftover chocolate by briefly melting it in the microwave oven at 50% power for 10 seconds, repeating until the chocolate is runny.

2. Dab some melted chocolate onto the back of each biscuit and press it onto the side of the cake, stacking a neat layer all round the sides.

3. Pile chocolate-dipped strawberries and chocolate hearts onto the top of the cake.

4. If you have not used a cake stand or serving plate, follow the method on p. 22: 'Decorating a cake board'.

Mini cakes ★

1. Use the leftover cake you have set aside, or any rectangular cake.

2. Cut the cake into squares the height of your biscuits and the width of two biscuits put together.

3. Cover your cakes with chocolate buttercream icing or dark chocolate ganache coating.

4. Dip the wafer biscuits into melted chocolate, as above, and let them set.

5. Dab melted chocolate onto the backs of the biscuits and press onto the sides of the mini cakes.

6. Decorate with strawberries and hearts.

Truffle tower

Truffles galore! A tower of truffles is a highly impressive dessert and delicious treat at a party. Guests will delight in picking off their own truffles from the tower.

Makes 50 – 60 servings at two truffles per person.

Truffles

You will need 100 – 120 truffles which you can buy, but why not make your own by tripling up the recipe on p. 146. Start making them weeks ahead of the party, saving costs and taking the pressure off your preparations.

Make the complete cake ★

Basis

To create the tower you need a basis onto which the truffles are attached. The easiest is to buy an Oasis® dry foam cone from a florist supplies shop. The cone should be 30 cm (12 in.) high and 12 cm (5 in.) in diameter.

You could also make your own cone using thick but pliable cardboard or a thick acetate sheet of 50 cm (20 in.) x 30 cm (12 in.).

1. Fold one side of the sheet over the other to form a cone.
2. Measure the open bottom from the shortest side for a diameter of 12 cm (5 in.). Stick the top corner down with adhesive tape.
3. Cut off the longer side at the bottom with scissors so that the cone will sit flat on a surface, with the apex in the centre. Staple all the edges together or stick with adhesive tape. If the cone were folded open, it would look similar to the photo.
4. Stuff the cardboard cone with newspaper to give it a solid structure.

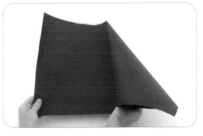

Assembling the truffle tower

1. Cover the basis, whether made from foam, cardboard or acetate, with plastic cling wrap.

2. Place the cone on a round 20 cm (8 in.) cake board, glass plate or cake stand.

3. Secure the sides of the cone to the board with adhesive tape.

4. Melt 300 g (10½ oz) dark chocolate according to the instructions on p. 15.

5. Using a pastry or paint brush, spread the melted chocolate onto the covered cone and cake board.

6. Dip each truffle in some melted chocolate and stick it to the chocolate-brushed surface, starting from the bottom and working your way up until you reach the top of the cone.

7. Pour 50 g (2 oz) melted white chocolate into a Ziploc bag and drip over the chocolate tower.

8. Decorate the cake with fresh flowers.

Mini truffle towers ★

For each mini tower you will need 10 truffles and a small 10 cm (4 in.) board or plate.

1. Place a truffle in the middle of the board, sticking it down with melted chocolate.

2. Place 5 truffles around the centre truffle, dipping the bottoms into the melted chocolate to stick them together.

3. Place 3 truffles dipped in chocolate on top of the bottom ring and finish with the last truffle on top.

Small shavings and bows

Small, individual cakes adorned with shavings and prettily striped bows are ideal for a small dinner or birthday party. These three make lovely centrepieces.

Serves 3 – 4 guests per cake or 9 – 12 guests in total.

Small shavings ★

1. Melt 150 g (5 oz) white chocolate (see instructions for melting on p. 15).
2. Colour with 5 ml (1 tsp) vegetable oil and 20 drops of liquid food colouring or some paste colouring using the colour of your choice, e.g. blue or turquoise.

This quantity of melted chocolate will make enough shavings to cover three cakes.

Method 1

1. Pour the melted, coloured chocolate onto a marble slab, stainless steel worktop, flat tile or thick rectangular glass plate.
2. Spread the chocolate, using a dough or metal scraper or a palette knife from side to side and keep on spreading from one side to the other. By keeping the chocolate moving, you regulate the temperature for the chocolate to set more evenly. Keep on spreading until the chocolate starts to thicken and set slightly.
3. Once it starts to set, quickly spread the chocolate flat into a thin layer.
4. While the chocolate sets, clean off the excess chocolate from the scraper and set it aside.
5. Wait until the chocolate is hard and solid before continuing. If the chocolate takes too long to set, lay a piece of clean plastic over the chocolate, put ice in a towel and press the towel on top of the plastic to cool down the chocolate. If you have used a marble slab, flat tile or glass plate, place this in the refrigerator for 10 minutes for the chocolate to set more quickly.
6. To form small shavings, push the scraper into the flat chocolate, away from your body at a 45° angle or pull a palette or large carving knife towards you at a 45° angle until shavings form. Scrape all the chocolate into shavings.

Method 2

1. Alternatively line a square cake tin or bread tin with plastic cling wrap or foil.

2. Pour the melted chocolate into the lined tin.

3. Let the chocolate rest until it becomes solid. This may take quite a while depending on the type of chocolate you have used, but do not refrigerate.

4. When the chocolate feels solid, turn out the block of chocolate and remove the wrap or foil.

5. Using a vegetable peeler, scrape the chocolate to form small rolls and shavings.

Striped chocolate bows ★★

Make half a batch of white chocolate paste (see recipe on p. 148). This quantity of paste is enough to make three bows.

To create paste with stripes

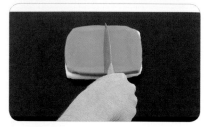

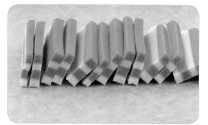

1. Divide the white chocolate paste in two. Colour one half of the paste with a few drops of food colouring according to your colour scheme, for example blue. Work the colour into the paste until it is uniform in colour.

2. Flatten each lump of paste on a piece of greaseproof paper or plastic cling wrap by rolling out with a rolling pin or glass bottle. Try to make two evenly-shaped square pieces of about 5 mm (⅕ in.) thick.

3. Sprinkle a few drops of cooled boiled water onto the flattened white paste. Place the flattened coloured paste on top of the first piece of flattened paste.

4. Cut the joined paste down the middle. Spread a few drops of cooled boiled water onto one half and place the other half on top.

5. Cover the block of paste with greaseproof paper or plastic cling wrap and let it rest in the refrigerator for 15 minutes to harden.

6. Take out the paste and cut it up into 15 even small blocks.

7. Turn each block on its side on greaseproof paper so that you can see the different layers forming stripes and roll it out with a rolling pin or glass bottle.

8. Cut each paste piece into an even rectangle with a sharp knife, pizza wheel or scissors and put the pieces in a plastic bag. You are now ready to start making the bows.

To create the bows

To make one bow, you will need 5 of the small paste rectangles.

1. Working on a tray lined with greaseproof paper, fold two pieces of paste over into loops. Place a piece of sponge, folded foil or folded paper towel into the loops to keep the shape.

2. Stick the loops together with some cooled, boiled water.

3. Fold a piece of paste over the middle where the loops meet.

4. Place two pieces of paste against each other to form the tail of the bow and fix these to the loops with water.

5. If the paste becomes too soft to mould, place the plastic bag with paste in the refrigerator for 5 minutes to harden.

6. Continue until all the bows have been formed. Let them harden before removing the plugs keeping the loops in shape.

Tips

- Keep your chocolate scrapings; they never go to waste but can be reused for attaching decorations to cakes or for making ganache or chocolate paste.
- The shavings can be stored in a dry, airtight container in a cool, dark cupboard for up to one month.
- The bows can be stored in an airtight container in a cupboard or in the refrigerator for up to two weeks.

Make the complete cake ★

- ✓ *1 rectangular sheet cake of 23 x 30 cm (9 x 12 in.), 5 cm (2 in.) high*
- ✓ *3 small square cake boards of 15 x 15 cm (6 x 6 in.). Use plywood, foamalite or cardboard cut to size and covered with aluminium foil.*
- ✓ *1 batch of white chocolate ganache coating (recipe p. 144)*
- ✓ *Chocolate shavings made with:*
     150 g (5 oz) white chocolate
     5 ml (1 tsp) vegetable oil
     20 drops of blue liquid food colouring or a few drops of turquoise paste colouring
- ✓ *Chocolate bows made with:*
     150 g (5 oz) white chocolate
     30 ml (2 tbsp) golden syrup or glucose syrup
     5 ml (1 tsp) water
     A few drops of liquid food colouring

Assembling the cake

1. If the rectangular cake is uneven on top, cut off the top crust very neatly by measuring the height of the cake layer with a ruler and pressing toothpicks into the cake at the height where you can level it. Using the toothpicks as a cutting guide, slice the cake above their tops.

2. Cut the cake into blocks with the following measurements:
   - 3 blocks measuring 10 x 10 cm (4 x 4 in.)
   - 3 blocks measuring 7.5 x 7.5 cm (3 x 3 in.)
   - 3 blocks measuring 5 x 5 cm (2 x 2 in.)

3. Do not discard the leftover cake. Freeze it and use it later for another project.

4. Spread each individual cake with white chocolate ganache coating.

5. Dollop some ganache between the layers to hold them in place and stack the tiers directly on each other without using sticks or boards in between the layers.

Tips

- Increase the quantities to make more cakes for larger functions.
- Paste cut-offs of the rectangular cake together with filling or coating to assemble more blocks.

Decorating the cake

1. Decorate one cake at a time. Using a hairdryer, slightly heat the ganache coating and press a handful of shavings onto all sides and on top of the cake.

2. Repeat until all the cakes are coated.

3. Decorate with chocolate bows attached with a dollop of ganache.

4. To decorate the cake boards, follow the method on p. 22.

Cupcakes ★

1. Spread ganache coating over the tops of your cupcakes until the coating is smooth.

2. Press some shavings into the ganache and place a chocolate bow on top.

Chocolate rose petal cake

Delicately light, flowery chocolate rose petals decorate this cake. When serving, cut the cake in half horizontally, dividing it into two cakes. Then cut each cake into thin slices and serve with a few petals for each guest.

Makes up to 16 servings.

Chocolate petals ★

100 g (3½ oz) of chocolate will make up to 25 petals. The quantity given here is for 75 petals.

1. Prepare baking tins or wooden trays which will fit into your refrigerator for making the petal decorations by cutting greaseproof paper to the size of each tray. Secure the paper by sticking it to the tray with adhesive tape or masking tape. If you line more than one tray with paper, it will be much quicker to make all the petals.

2. If working with eating chocolate only, you can put the trays in the refrigerator for 20 minutes before making your decorations on them to help the chocolate set more quickly.

3. Melt 300 g (10½ oz) white chocolate (see instructions for melting chocolate on p. 15).

4. Divide the chocolate into two bowls, keeping them warm on a towel on a warming tray or periodically remelting the chocolate in the microwave oven at 50% power for a few seconds at a time.

5. Colour one half of the melted white chocolate with 2.5 ml (½ tsp) vegetable oil mixed with 6 drops (⅛ tsp) of red or pink liquid food colouring or use 2 or more drops of paste food colouring (see instructions for colouring chocolate on p. 17).

6. To create a marbling effect, take a third bowl and swirl some of the coloured and some of the white chocolate together. Do not over-mix the two colours. Keep the rest of the chocolate at hand and use a little at a time.

7. To start making the petals, dip one side of your palette knife into the marbled chocolate and dab the dollop of chocolate onto the paper on the tray. Slide towards you and lift to shape a petal. The rounded side of the palette knife forms the top of the petal.

8. Try to form even-sized shapes by lifting the palette knife after a 5 cm (2 in.) long smear. Repeat until you have filled the paper with petals.

9. Put the tray with the chocolate in the refrigerator for no longer than 10 minutes, just to let the chocolate cool and set completely.

10. Remove the trays from the refrigerator and carefully peel the chocolate petals from the paper.

How many petals should you make?

You do not want to be caught with too few petals to cover your cake, nor do you want to waste time making unnecessary petals. You can work out very precisely how many petals you will need.

1. The width of one petal is the width of your palette knife, normally 3 cm (1¼ in.). Measure your palette knife to find the width of your petals.

2. Measure the circumference of your cake and divide by the width of each petal (i.e. your palette knife). This gives you the number of petals you need to go round the cake in one layer (e.g. if the cake is 65 cm (26 in.) all round, divide by 3 cm (1¼ in.) = about 21 petals in a layer).

3. Measure the height of your cake and divide by the height of each petal (i.e. how long you made the smear). This gives you the number of layers you need to cover the entire cake (e.g. if the cake is 15 cm (6 in.) high, divide by 5 cm (2 in.) high petals = 3 layers).

4. Now multiply the number of petals with the number of layers and you know exactly how many petals will cover the whole cake (e.g. 21 x 3 = 63). Always make a few more petals in case some break.

Big chocolate paste rose and petals ★★

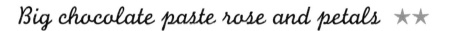

1. Make a batch of white chocolate paste from the recipe on p. 148. Divide the paste in half and colour each with a few drops of red or pink food colouring until you have two different shades of pink: a light and a darker pink.

2. Break off a piece of the light pink paste the size of a ping pong ball or about 30 g (1 oz) and roll it between your palms into a cone shape. This will form the heart of the rose.

3. Place the cone on a piece of greaseproof paper and let it set in the refrigerator for 5 minutes.

4. Divide the rest of the light pink paste into 8 evenly-sized pieces of about 20 g (¾ oz) each and roll them into balls between your palms.

5. Use icing sugar (confectioner's sugar) to dust your hands if the paste feels sticky.

6. Flatten each ball by pinching it between your fingers or by placing it on grease-proof paper and pressing with your fingers, a rolling pin or a glass bottle.

7. To make life-like petals, pinch the top edges between your fingers to flatten and thin them. Pinch an indent in middle of each petal to resemble a rose petal.

8. Wrap the first petal tightly around the cone, to cover the cone, slightly curling the petal open. If it doesn't stick, use a few drops of cooled boiled water to act as glue.

9. Attach a second petal to the cone, opposite the first one, also slightly curling the petal open. Try to tuck the petals underneath each other to look more realistic.

10. Add the rest of the petals, one at a time, until you have a full rose which can form the centrepiece of your cake.

11. Use the darker pink paste to make 10 more evenly-sized petals of about 20 g (¾ oz) each. These are used to cover the top of your cake, making it look as if your rose has shed some petals!

Tips

- Whenever the paste feels too soft for shaping or becomes difficult to handle, cover with plastic cling wrap and place in the refrigerator for 5 minutes to harden slightly.
- Slightly curling open each petal creates an open rose, while standing them more vertically creates a tighter rose. Three petals wrapped around the centre cone make a lovely rosebud, five petals form a normal rose, and seven or more petals create a very large rose.
- The rose and petals can be made up to two weeks ahead and stored in an airtight container in a cool, dark cupboard or in the refrigerator.

Mini cakes ★

1. Remove the paper wrappers from your cupcakes and stick two cupcakes together with chocolate ganache filling.

2. Cut slivers from the sides of the mini cake to make it even all round.

3. Coat the mini cakes with buttercream icing or white chocolate ganache coating.

4. Dab melted chocolate on the backs of chocolate petals and press onto the cakes, working from the top downwards.

5. Place a small chocolate paste rose on top of each mini cake.

Make the complete cake ★

- ✓ 3 round cake layers of 15 cm (6 in.) in diameter and 5 cm (2 in.) high
- ✓ 1 round 25 cm (10 in.) cake board, plywood board or cake stand
- ✓ Wooden skewer
- ✓ 1 batch of plain buttercream icing (recipe p. 140) or 1 batch each of white chocolate ganache filling and coating (recipes p. 142 and p. 144)
- ✓ Chocolate petals made with:
  - 300 g (1¼ lb) white chocolate
  - 2.5 ml (½ tsp) vegetable oil
  - 6 drops (⅛ tsp) of red or pink liquid food colouring or 2 or more drops of paste food colouring
- ✓ Chocolate paste rose and petals made with:
  - 300 g (10½ oz) white chocolate
  - 60 ml (4 tbsp) golden syrup or glucose syrup
  - 10 ml (2 tsp) water
- ✓ 100 g (3½ oz) white chocolate melted, for attaching the petals to the cake

Note: The cake in this project is about 15 cm (6 in.) high. If your cake is smaller or larger, adjust the amounts of buttercream or ganache and chocolate needed.

Assembling the cake

1. Place one layer of cake on the cake board or stand. Fill each layer with buttercream icing or chocolate ganache filling, and stack them on top of one another.

2. Push a wooden skewer right through the centre of all the layers and cut it off level with the top of the cake (see p. 21 for stacking cakes). This will keep the cakes in place and will carry the weight of the big chocolate paste rose.

3. Coat the whole cake with plain buttercream icing or white chocolate ganache coating.

Decorating the cake

1. Melt the white chocolate according to the instructions on p. 15. Pour into a zip-lock bag and snip off one corner to make a piping bag.

2. Starting from the top edge of the cake, cover the cake with chocolate petals by piping some melted chocolate on the back of each petal and sticking it onto the cake.

3. From the top of the cake work downwards, sticking the petals over each other and overlapping where necessary, until you reach the bottom of the cake.

4. If the chocolate in the zip-lock bag starts to set, heat the bag in the microwave oven at 50% power for 10 seconds. Repeat until the chocolate is runny.

5. Place the big rose in the middle of the cake.

6. Press the dark pink petals into the top of the cake around the rose.

7. Follow the method on p. 22: 'Decorating a cake board'.

Square spirals cake

This is an easy cake for a beginner to make: it looks impressive but is fairly quick to make. When serving, cut this cake in half horizontally so that you have two cakes and then cut each cake into squares.

Makes up to 30 servings.

Chocolate paste spirals ★

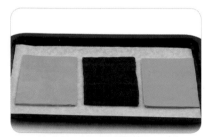

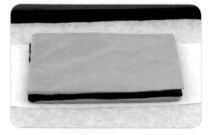

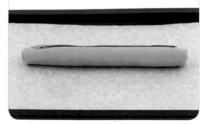

1. Make a batch of white chocolate paste from the recipe on p. 148. Divide the paste in two and colour each half with a few drops of food colouring according to your colour scheme, for example blue and green. Work the colour into the paste until it is uniform in colour.

2. Make dark chocolate paste from the recipe on p. 148 using only half the ingredients to make half a batch.

3. Flatten each lump of paste on a piece of greaseproof paper or plastic cling wrap by rolling out with a rolling pin or glass bottle. Try to make three evenly-shaped rectangular pieces of about 5 mm (⅕ in.) thick.

4. Sprinkle a few drops of cooled boiled water onto one piece of flattened paste. Turn another piece of paste over and place it on top of the first piece. Sprinkle some more water onto the second piece of flattened paste and place the third piece on top.

You now have a choice: If you want big spirals, proceed with the next step, but if you want medium-sized decorations with more spiral patterns, see step 6).

5. Sprinkle more water over the last piece of flattened paste and, using your hands, roll the rectangle consisting of three colours together into a thick sausage with the help of the greaseproof paper or plastic cling wrap on which you are working.

6. If you want more spiral patterns and smaller spirals, first roll the thick rectangle with its three colours slightly flatter with a rolling pin or glass bottle before rolling it into a sausage shape.

7. Wrap the sausage of paste in the paper or plastic cling wrap and let it rest in the refrigerator for 30 minutes to harden.

8. Using a sharp knife and a cutting board, cut off slices from half of the sausage. If the chocolate sausage is too hard, wait for it to soften slightly before cutting or heat the knife in boiling water, thoroughly drying it before cutting.

9. To vary the size of the spirals, roll the rest of the sausage into a narrower shape with your hands and place it back in the refrigerator for 10 minutes to harden.

10. Slice the rest of the sausage into round pieces with a sharp knife.

11. Push a toothpick into some of the thicker spirals to use on top of the cake.

Tips

- Using latex gloves to mix food colouring into the paste will protect your hands from getting stained. Latex gloves are also useful when kneading the paste as the paste doesn't stick to the gloves.
- The chocolate paste spirals can be made up to two weeks ahead and stored in an airtight container in the refrigerator.

Cupcakes ★

- Spread the tops of your cupcakes with buttercream icing or chocolate ganache coating.
- Push spirals on toothpicks into the top of each cupcake.

Make the complete cake ★

✓ 3 square cake layers of 15 x 15 cm (6 x 6 in.), each 5 cm (2 in.) high, preferably white cake such as the white chocolate mud cake on p. 126

Tip

You could bake one cake of 30 cm (12 in.) square and cut it up to assemble a block of cake 15 cm (6 in.) square.

✓ 1 square 25 x 25 cm (10 x 10 in.) cake board, plywood board or cake stand
✓ Wooden skewer
✓ 1½ batch of plain buttercream icing (recipe p. 140) or 1½ batch each of white chocolate ganache filling and coating (recipes p. 142 and p. 144)
✓ Chocolate paste spirals made with:
   1 recipe white chocolate paste:
      300 g (10½ oz) white chocolate
      60 ml (4 tbsp) golden syrup or glucose syrup
      10 ml (2 tsp) water
   ½ recipe dark chocolate paste:
      150 g (5¼ oz) dark chocolate
      37.5 ml (2½ tbsp) golden syrup or glucose syrup
      5 ml (1 tsp) water
✓ 100 g (3½ oz) white chocolate melted, for attaching the decorations

Note: The cake in this project is about 15 cm (6 in.) high. If your cake is smaller or larger, adjust the amounts of buttercream or ganache and chocolate needed.

Assembling and decorating the cake

1. Place one layer of cake on the cake board or stand. Fill each layer with plain buttercream icing or chocolate ganache filling, stacking them on top of one another.

2. Push a wooden skewer right through the centre of all the layers and cut it off level with the top of the cake (see p. 21 for stacking cakes).

3. Coat the whole cake with plain buttercream icing or white ganache coating.

4. Pour the 100 g (3½ oz) melted white chocolate into a zip-lock bag and snip off one corner to make a piping bag.

5. Decorate the cake by piping some melted chocolate onto the back of each spiral and pressing it onto the cake. Start at the top of the cake and work your way down.

6. Push some of the spirals on toothpicks into the top of the cake.

7. If you have not used a cake stand or serving plate, follow the method on p. 22: 'Decorating a cake board'.

Spiky cake

The sharp and curly edges of these spiky triangles are quite modern and funky!

Makes up to 20 servings.

Spiky chocolate triangles

The following instructions produce 150 triangles. To adjust the amounts, remember that every 100 g (3½ oz) of chocolate will yield 25 triangles.

1. Place a piece of greaseproof paper on a baking tin or wooden tray that will fit into your refrigerator and secure the edges of the paper by sticking it to the tray with adhesive tape or masking tape. If working with eating chocolate only, you can put the tray in the refrigerator for 20 minutes before using it.

2. Cut strips of greaseproof paper of approximately 7.5 cm (3 in.) wide and 50 cm (20 in.) long. Cut these strips diagonally into 150 triangles altogether.

3. Melt two batches of white chocolate according to the instructions on p. 15 and colour them according to the instructions on p. 17, namely:
   – 300 g (10½ oz) white chocolate coloured with 5 ml (1 tsp) vegetable oil mixed with your choice of colour (e.g. 10 drops of red or pink liquid food colouring or 5 drops of paste food colouring)
   – and 300 g (10½ oz) white chocolate coloured with 5 ml (1 tsp) vegetable oil mixed with your choice of colour (e.g. lime green created by mixing 8 drops of yellow with 2 drops of green liquid food colouring, or 5 drops of paste food colouring).

4. Pour a teaspoonful of the first batch of coloured chocolate onto a triangle. Spread the chocolate with the back of the spoon. Repeat with more triangles.

5. Let the chocolate set slightly before lifting each triangle with a knife and placing it on its side, upright, on the tray. The triangle's point can bend and curl slightly, creating unevenly shaped spikes, which is the look you want to create.

6. If you want less curly triangles, place them over a glass bottle. Secure the sides of the bottle with Prestik (Blu-Tack) to keep it from rolling.

7. If the chocolate starts to set on the sides of the bowl, reheat in a microwave oven at 20% power or on the defrost setting. Periodically scrape the hardened chocolate from your worktop and remelt to make more triangles.

8. Place the tray in the refrigerator for 10 minutes until the chocolate has set. Then remove from the refrigerator and pull off the paper from the chocolate. Set the triangles aside for later use.

9. Repeat the steps with the next colour of chocolate.

Tip

To make the exact number of triangles you will need for your cake, you can make the templates in the following way:

1. Measure the height and the circumference of each tier of the cake. Normally the height for each tier will be the same but the circumferences will differ.

2. Add 5 cm (2 in.) to the height measurement and 5 cm (2 in.) to each circumference measurement.

3. Cut a strip of greaseproof paper for each tier as wide as the new height measurement and as long as the new circumference measurement.

4. Now cut each strip in half lengthways into two long strips and cut all the strips into triangles. The triangles can be different in width and do not have to be exact, but there will be enough to cover your cake.

Mini cakes ★

1. Remove the paper wrappers from your cupcakes and stick two cupcakes together with filling.

2. Refrigerate the filled cupcakes for an hour to make them easier to cut.

3. Turn the filled cupcakes upside down so that the narrowest part is on top and cut slivers from the sides of each mini cake to give it a slight pyramid shape.

4. Coat the mini cakes with buttercream icing or white chocolate ganache coating.

5. Decorate them with triangles stuck on with melted chocolate.

Make the complete cake ★★

✓ 3 round cakes (each 2 layers) of decreasing sizes: 15 cm (6 in.), 10 cm (4 in.) and 5 cm (2 in.) in diameter

Tip

The layers of the 10 cm (4 in.) and 5 cm (2 in.) cakes can be cut from a single-layer 20 cm (8 in.) square cake.

✓ 1 round 25 cm (10 in.) cake board, plywood board or cake stand
✓ 1 batch of plain buttercream icing (recipe p. 140) or 1 batch each of white chocolate ganache filling and coating (recipes p. 142 and p. 144)
✓ Chocolate triangles made with:
    600 g (1¼ lb) white chocolate
    10 ml (2 tsp) vegetable oil
    Liquid or paste food colouring
✓ 100 g (3½ oz) white chocolate melted, for attaching the triangles to the cake
✓ Fresh flowers, e.g. green chrysanthemums

Note: This three-tiered cake is about 30 cm (12 in.) high. If your cake is smaller or larger, adjust the amounts of buttercream or ganache and chocolate needed.

Assembling and decorating the cake

1. Divide each layer into two (see instructions on p. 19: 'Filling and coating cakes'). Fill and assemble each cake with either plain buttercream icing or white chocolate ganache filling.

2. Place the largest cake on the cake board. As the cakes are not too heavy, you can now proceed to stack the tiers without using a board or plate between the layers. Just put a dollop of buttercream or ganache between each tier. Place the next size cake directly on the largest cake and the smallest on top. It is also not necessary to put a wooden skewer through all the layers.

3. Refrigerate or freeze your cake for an hour. This will make it easier to cut.

4. Slightly trim the sharp edges of the layers to give the cake a step-pyramid shape.

5. Coat the whole cake with the remaining buttercream icing or white ganache coating.

6. Melt 100 g (3½ oz) white chocolate, pour into a zip-lock bag and snip off a corner to make a piping bag.

7. Pipe some chocolate onto the back of each triangle before pressing it onto the cake. Start from the top tier, working your way down to the bottom tier.

8. Overlap triangles where necessary.

9. If you have not used a cake stand or serving plate, follow the method on p. 22: 'Decorating a cake board' and add fresh flowers to the cake.

Pleated cake with filigree decorations

This cake makes a fashion statement with its pleated fabric look!

Makes up to 50 servings.

Pleated chocolate paste ★★

1. Make four times the normal batch of white chocolate paste from the recipe on p. 148. Colour it with liquid food colouring according to your colour scheme, for example pink. Work the colour into the paste until it is uniform in colour. Using latex gloves when colouring the paste will protect your hands from getting stained. If the paste feels too soft after colouring, cover it with plastic wrap and put it into a refrigerator for 15 minutes to set and harden.

2. Place a piece of greaseproof paper on a baking tin (sheet) or wooden tray that will fit into your refrigerator and secure the edges of the paper to the tray with adhesive tape or masking tape.

3. Take medium-sized pieces of paste of about 30 g (1 oz) and roll them into sausages.

4. Flatten the sausages by placing them between two pieces of greaseproof paper or plastic cling wrap or inside a large zip-lock bag and rolling them out with a rolling pin or glass bottle. The paste must be rolled out until very thin. If you have a pasta roller, put the sausages through that. Roll the paste as high as your cake.

5. If the paste sticks to the paper or plastic, place in the refrigerator for 5 minutes to harden.

6. Pull the flattened paste off the paper and pleat it with your fingers or place it over four wooden skewers to resemble pleated fabric.

7. Place the pleated paste on the prepared tray. Continue making pleated paste pieces until the tray is full and then place it in the refrigerator for the paste to harden. You can keep the pleats in the refrigerator until you're ready to use them on your cake.

8. Repeat until all the paste has been used.

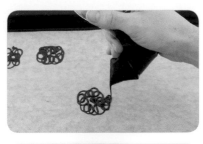

Chocolate filigrees ★

1. Place a piece of greaseproof paper on a baking tin (sheet) or wooden tray that will fit into your refrigerator and secure the edges of the paper by sticking it to the tray with adhesive tape or masking tape. If working with eating chocolate only, you can put the tray in the refrigerator for 20 minutes before using it.

2. Melt 100 g (3½ oz) dark chocolate (see instructions on p. 15). Pour the melted chocolate into a zip-lock bag and snip off one corner to make a piping bag.

3. Pipe free-hand filigree patterns onto the paper.

4. When the paper has been covered with piped filigree decorations, place the tray in the refrigerator for 10 minutes for the chocolate to set.

5. Remove the tray from the refrigerator and pull the filigree decorations off the paper or carefully slide a palette knife underneath each decoration.

6. Repeat the steps until all the melted chocolate has been used. If the chocolate in the piping bag starts to set, you can remelt it by placing the bag in the microwave oven and heating it at 50% power for 10-second intervals.

Tip

The filigree decorations can be made up to two weeks ahead and stored in an airtight container in a cool, dark cupboard.

Make the complete cake ★★

✓ 3 square cakes (each 2 layers) of different sizes: 20 x 20 cm (8 x 8 in.), 15 x 15 cm (6 x 6 in.) and 10 x 10 cm (4 x 4 in.)

✓ 1 square 30 cm (12 in.) cake board, plywood board or cake stand

✓ 1 square 15 cm (6 in.) divider made from thick cardboard or foamalite, wrapped in aluminium foil or plastic cling wrap

✓ 2 batches of plain or chocolate buttercream icing (recipe p. 140) or 2 batches each of white or dark chocolate ganache filling and coating (recipes p. 142 and p. 144)

✓ Chocolate paste pleated fabric made from four batches of white chocolate paste (recipe p. 148) coloured dark pink, made with:
>   1.2 kg (2 lb 10 oz) white chocolate, melted (see method p. 148)
>   250 ml (9 fl oz/1 cup) golden syrup or glucose syrup
>   40 ml (8 tsp) water
>   Food colouring

✓ 100 g (3½ oz) white or dark chocolate, melted, to attach decorations

✓ Dark chocolate filigrees made with 100 g (3½ oz) dark chocolate

Tips

• The layers of the 15 cm (6 in.) and 10 cm (4 in.) square cakes can be cut from one single-layer rectangular sheet cake of 23 x 30 cm (9 x 12 in.), giving you a slightly smaller top tier of 8 cm (3 in.).

• Alternatively the layers of the 10 cm (4 in.) square cake could be cut from two extra 15 cm (6 in.) square cake layers.

Note: This three-tiered cake is about 30 cm (12 in.) high. If your cake is smaller or larger, adjust the amounts of buttercream or ganache and chocolate needed.

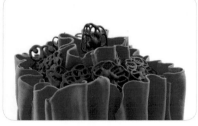

Assembling and decorating the cake

1. Divide the layers (see instructions on p. 19: 'Filling and coating cakes'). Fill and coat each cake with either buttercream icing or chocolate ganache.

2. Place the largest cake on the cake board. Put wooden skewers into the bottom cake as per the instructions on p. 21, to take the weight of the other tiers.

3. Place the next largest cake on foamalite or cardboard as a separator and centre it on the bottom tier.

4. Use a dollop of buttercream or ganache to place the next tier directly on top of the others. The small cake does not need a board as it is not very heavy.

5. Pour the 100 g (3½ oz) melted white or dark chocolate into a zip-lock bag and snip off a corner to make a piping bag.

6. Pipe some chocolate onto the back of each pleat before pressing it onto the cake or pipe the chocolate directly onto the cake before pressing the pleat onto the cake. Start from the top of the cake, working your way down to the bottom. Overlap pleats where necessary.

7. Add chocolate filigrees to the top of each cake tier.

8. If you have not used a cake stand or serving plate, follow the method on p. 22: 'Decorating a cake board'.

Mini cakes ★★

1. Remove the paper wrappers from your cupcakes and stick two cupcakes together with filling.

2. Cover the mini cakes with buttercream icing or chocolate ganache coating.

3. Use melted chocolate to attach chocolate pleats around the outside.

4. Add chocolate filigrees to the top of each mini cake.

Shards and Christmas trees

This easy-to-make Christmas cake is a good alternative to a traditional cake, especially if the chocolate fruitcake recipe is used. It will make a lasting impression on your family and friends.

Makes up to 30 servings.

Chocolate shards ★

You can let your imagination run wild when designing the decorative pattern for these delicious shards.

1. Make templates by cutting 2 pieces of greaseproof paper into rectangles of approximately 25 cm (10 in.) wide and 50 cm (20 in.) long.

2. Place the templates on two baking or wooden trays that will fit into your refrigerator and secure the ends with adhesive tape. If working with eating chocolate only, you can refrigerate the trays for 20 minutes for a cool surface to work on.

3. Melt 100 g (3½ oz) white chocolate according to the instructions on p. 15 and colour according to the instructions on p. 17 using your choice of colour, e.g. 2.5 ml (½ tsp) oil mixed with 10 drops of green liquid food colouring or 2 – 5 drops of paste food colouring.

4. Pour the melted, coloured chocolate into a Ziploc bag and snip off a corner to make a piping bag.

5. Pipe a pattern of coloured chocolate onto the templates. Use stripes or squiggles or even numbers and letters of the alphabet, but remember: they will be mirror images as they are turned over! Wait until the chocolate sets slightly, otherwise your designs will smudge.

6. Melt 450 g (1 lb) dark or milk chocolate (see instructions on p. 15). Pour half the melted chocolate in a thick line onto one of the templates over the patterns.

7. Quickly spread the chocolate with a palette knife from side to side and keep on spreading from one side to the other. By keeping the chocolate moving, you regulate the temperature for the chocolate to set more evenly. It does not matter if the chocolate spreads over the edges of the paper. Keep on spreading until the chocolate starts to thicken and set slightly.

8. Repeat with the rest of the chocolate and the other template.

9. Touch the surface of the chocolate with your finger. If the chocolate is slightly firm, without chocolate coming off onto your finger, it is ready to be cut.

10. Use a pizza wheel or sharp knife to cut the sheet of chocolate in half lengthwise so that the shards will be slightly higher than the cake itself.

11. Place the trays with chocolate in the refrigerator, for no longer than 10 minutes, to let the chocolate cool and set completely.

12. Remove the chocolate from the refrigerator and lift it off the paper. Carefully break off big pieces of chocolate shards. To make it easier to break, make cuts with a knife here and there. Remember to snap the chocolate immediately after removing it from the refrigerator, before it can become soft again.

Tip

To make the exact quantity of shards you will need to cover your cake, you can make a template in the following way:

1. Measure the width of one side of the square cake. Add 5 cm (2 in.) to this measurement.

2. Measure the height of the cake. Add 2.5 cm (1 in.) to this measurement.

3. Cut two rectangular pieces of greaseproof paper, each as long as double the width measurement and double as wide as the height measurement.

4. Place the papers on baking tins or wooden trays that will fit into your refrigerator and use adhesive tape or masking tape to make a handle for each end and to keep the paper in place.

Cupcakes ★

Spread the top of your cupcakes with chocolate ganache coating or buttercream icing and press a chocolate Christmas tree onto the top of each cupcake.

Chocolate Christmas trees ★

1. Copy the tree template on p. 157 on paper several times, setting the trees far apart to accommodate wooden skewers which will be used to position the Christmas trees upright in your cake. Place these drawings on a baking tin (sheet) or wooden tray that will fit into your refrigerator.

2. Cut see-through greaseproof paper to line the tray prepared with your tree template, place over the template and secure the paper by sticking it to the tray with adhesive tape or masking tape. If working with eating chocolate only, you can put the tray in the refrigerator for 20 minutes before making your decorations on it.

3. Melt 100 g (3½ oz) white chocolate according to the instructions on p. 15 and colour according to the instructions on p. 17 with 2.5 ml (½ tsp) oil mixed with 10 drops of green liquid food colouring or 2 – 5 drops of paste food colouring.

4. Pour the coloured chocolate into a Ziploc bag and snip off a corner to make a piping bag.

5. Place a wooden skewer in position on your template as the trunk for a Christmas tree and, following the design, pipe an outline of a tree onto the paper with the coloured, melted chocolate.

6. Fill in the rest of the tree with the chocolate.

7. Repeat with the other trees until the tray is full.

8. As the chocolate starts to set, use a toothpick to make random branch-like markings by placing it into the setting chocolate and quickly pulling it out again.

9. Place the tray in the refrigerator for 10 minutes for the chocolate to set.

10. Decorate the Christmas trees:
    – Pipe a few dots of melted chocolate onto half of the finished trees and randomly place gold dragees onto the piped dots.
    – Pipe some melted chocolate onto the other half of the trees and pour a pinch of white nonpareils over to resemble snow.

11. Let the decorations set completely before taking hold of the wooden skewers and peeling the chocolate trees from the paper.

Make the complete cake ★

✓ 1 square cake (2 layers) of 20 x 20 cm (8 x 8 in.)
✓ 1 square 30 x 30 cm (12 x 12 in.) cake board, plywood board or cake stand
✓ 1¼ batch of chocolate buttercream icing (recipe p. 141) or 1¼ batch each of dark or milk chocolate ganache filling and coating (recipes p. 142 and p. 144)
✓ Chocolate shards made with:
    450 g (1 lb) dark or milk chocolate
    100 g (3½ oz) white chocolate
    2.5 ml (½ tsp) vegetable oil
    10 drops of green liquid food colouring
✓ 100 g (3½ oz) dark or milk chocolate melted, to attach shards
✓ Chocolate Christmas trees made with:
    100 g (3½ oz) white chocolate
    2.5 ml (½ tsp) vegetable oil
    10 drops of green liquid food colouring
✓ White nonpareils
✓ Gold dragees (candy beads)
✓ Wooden skewers

Note: This cake is about 10 cm (4 in.) high. If your cake is smaller or larger, adjust the amounts of buttercream or ganache and chocolate needed.

Assembling and decorating the cake

1. Divide each cake into two layers (see instructions on p. 19: 'Filling and coating cakes'). Fill the layers with chocolate buttercream icing or ganache filling.

2. Place on the cake board and cover with the rest of the buttercream icing or ganache coating.

3. Melt 100 g (3½ oz) dark or milk chocolate. Use a palette knife or teaspoon to spread some melted chocolate onto the back of each shard before pressing it onto the cake.

4. Add chocolate Christmas trees to the top of the cake.

5. If you have not used a cake stand or serving plate, follow the method on p. 22: 'Decorating a cake board'.

Retro polka dot collar

Pink and polka dots remind you of a baby girl; bake this cake with its modern twist for a baby shower or christening. Colour the chocolate blue for a baby boy.

Makes up to 24 servings.

Polka dot collar ★★

A template, which will fit snugly around your cake, is cut and the melted chocolate is poured onto this. When it has set slightly but is still pliable, the collar is fitted around your cake.

1. To make a template, measure the height and circumference of your cake. Add 2.5 cm (1 in.) to the height and 5 cm (2 in.) to the circumference and cut a piece of greaseproof paper to this new measurement.
2. Place the paper on a flat surface and use adhesive tape or masking tape to make a handle for each end and to keep the paper in place.
3. Melt 50 g (2 oz) dark chocolate, pour into a Ziploc bag and snip off a corner to make a piping bag.
4. Pipe dots of dark chocolate onto the paper varying the sizes or, if you prefer, keeping them all the same size. Wait until the chocolate sets slightly, otherwise the polka dots will smudge.
5. Melt 450 g (1 lb) white chocolate and colour it with 5 ml (1 tsp) vegetable oil mixed with 15 drops (¼ tsp) of your choice of food colouring, e.g. red or pink.
6. Pour the coloured chocolate onto the paper over the polka dots in a thick line.

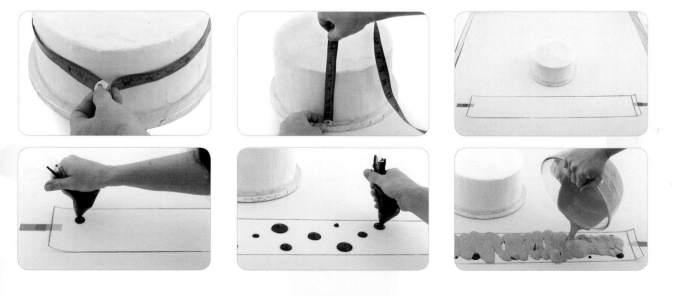

7. Quickly spread the chocolate with a palette knife from side to side and keep spreading from one side to the other. Keep a 2.5 cm (1 in.) strip of paper open on one side by which you will later pick up the template. Spread the chocolate over the edges of the paper because the chocolate on the edges always sets more quickly than the chocolate in the middle. By keeping the chocolate moving, you regulate the temperature for the chocolate to set more evenly. Keep on spreading until the chocolate starts to thicken and set slightly. If you are using eating chocolate only, this step may take up to 30 minutes.

8. Now comes the tricky part, where you have to judge whether the chocolate has set enough to stay in one piece yet is still pliable enough to be lifted and bent. Touch the surface of the chocolate with your finger. If the chocolate is slightly firm but still warm, with some chocolate coming off onto your finger, the collar is ready to be lifted.

9. Quickly lift the paper off the work surface by holding the clean strip at one end and the adhesive tape at the other end. Press the collar onto the cake with the chocolate side against the cake and the paper on the outside.

10. Use your hands to guide the paper all the way around the cake and fold one edge over the other.

11. Place the cake in the refrigerator for no longer than 10 minutes, just to let the chocolate cool and set completely.

12. Scrape all leftover hardened chocolate from your worktop into a Ziploc bag to use in another project or for making ganache filling or coating.

13. To complete the cake, see the instructions for the full project.

Tip

Why stop at polka dots? You could also decorate the collar with the baby's initials in melted chocolate, but do remember that you get a mirror image, as the collar is used the other way round! Slide a piece of paper with your reverse design under the grease-proof paper template and pipe the design in melted chocolate.

Chocolate spirals ★

1. Cut a piece of greaseproof paper to line a baking or wooden tray that will fit into your refrigerator. Secure the paper with adhesive tape. If working with eating chocolate only, you can place the tray in the refrigerator for 20 minutes before making your decorations on it.

2. Melt 50 g (2 oz) dark chocolate, pour into a Ziploc bag and snip off a corner to make a piping bag.

3. Pipe free-hand spirals onto the paper. Wait for it to set slightly otherwise it will smudge.

4. Melt 50 g (2 oz) white chocolate and colour with 1.25 ml (¼ tsp) vegetable oil mixed with 2 drops of liquid food colouring of your choice, e.g. red or pink. Pour the melted, coloured chocolate into a Ziploc bag and snip off a corner to make a piping bag.

5. Pipe dots of coloured chocolate over the spirals.

6. When the tray has been filled, place it in the refrigerator for 10 minutes for the chocolate to set.

7. Peel the spiral decorations off the paper or carefully slide a palette knife underneath each decoration.

8. Repeat the steps until all the melted chocolate has been used.

Make the complete cake ★★

- ✓ 1 round cake (2 layers) of 20 cm (8 in.)
- ✓ 1 round 30 cm (12 in.) cake board, plywood board, glass plate or cake stand
- ✓ 1 batch plain buttercream icing (recipe p. 140) or 1 batch each of white chocolate ganache filling and coating (recipes p. 142 and p. 144)
- ✓ Chocolate polka dot collar made with:
  - 50 g (2 oz) dark chocolate
  - 450 g (1 lb) white chocolate
  - 5 ml (1 tsp) vegetable oil
  - 15 drops (¼ tsp) of red or pink liquid food colouring
- ✓ Chocolate spirals made with:
  - 50 g (2 oz) dark chocolate
  - 50 g (2 oz) white chocolate
  - 1.25 ml (¼ tsp) vegetable oil
  - 2 drops of red or pink liquid food colouring
- ✓ 20 truffles (use bought truffles or make your own from the recipe on p. 146)

Assembling and decorating the cake

1. Divide the layers, fill and coat your cake and place it on its board. (See instructions on p. 19: 'Filling and coating cakes'.)

2. Measure the height and circumference and make the greaseproof paper template as described in the instructions for the collar.

3. Pipe the polka dots and proceed to make the collar.

4. When the fitted collar has set, carefully remove the paper. Where the ends of the paper meet, slowly wriggle out the paper from under the top chocolate seam.

5. With a sharp knife or pizza wheel, carefully cut off the overlapping chocolate seam so that the two ends meet neatly.

6. Dab some melted chocolate on the inside of the collar where the seam meets, to seal the join.

7. For an extra decorative touch, pipe some of the leftover coloured chocolate over the truffles if you prefer, and add them to the cake.

8. Add the chocolate spirals to the top of the cake.

9. If you have not used a cake stand or serving plate, decorate your cake board, following the method on p. 22: 'Decorating a cake board'.

Mini cakes ★★

1. Remove the paper wrappers from your cupcakes and stick two cupcakes together with filling.

2. Place the mini cakes in the refrigerator for an hour, making them easier to cut.

3. Slice a sliver from all sides to make the mini cakes even all round.

4. Cover with buttercream icing or ganache coating.

5. Take the measurements of one mini cake and use that to make templates for all of them.

6. Make chocolate collars as described on p. 81: 'Individual cakes'.

7. Place a small chocolate collar around each mini cake and decorate with a chocolate spiral and truffle on top.

Ice cream scoops

The plain chocolate icing sets off the brightly coloured chocolate scoops beautifully; this birthday cake will be a hit at any age!

Makes up to 60 servings.

Ice cream scoops ★★

- Use an ice cream scoop to create these delicious curls.
- 100 g (3½ oz) of chocolate makes ±15 curls.
- The following instructions use 800 g (1¾ lb) chocolate to make 120 curls.

1. Melt four batches of white chocolate of 200 g (7 oz) each, i.e. 800 g (1¾ lb) altogether.

2. Colour the four batches in the colour scheme you prefer, mixing the food colouring with 2.5 ml (½ tsp) vegetable oil each time, e.g.:

   – Purple: mix 8 drops of blue with 2 drops of red liquid food colouring or use 2 drops of paste food colouring.

   – Blue: 10 drops of blue liquid food colouring or 2 drops of turquoise paste food colouring.

   – Red: 10 drops of red liquid food colouring or 1.25 ml (¼ tsp) red powder colouring or 2 drops of red paste food colouring.

   – Yellow: 10 drops of yellow liquid food colouring.

3. Working with one colour of chocolate at a time, pour the melted chocolate onto a marble slab, flat tile, thick rectangular glass plate, stainless steel worktop or granite worktop. (If the marble slab, tile or glass plate becomes too hot and the chocolate doesn't set quickly enough, refrigerate it until it feels cooler. If using a stainless steel or granite worktop, use different parts of the worktop to pour the chocolate onto.)

4. Scrape the chocolate from side to side with a dough or metal scraper or palette knife until it cools slightly and becomes thicker.

5. When the chocolate starts to set, spread it flat into a thick layer. The thicker you spread the chocolate, the bigger your curls will be.

6. While waiting for the chocolate to cool and set, clean the excess chocolate off the scraper, with a sharp knife, for reuse.

7. Press your finger onto the chocolate: if it still feels slightly warm but does not leave a fingerprint, it is ready to use.

8. To form ice cream scoops, push the ice cream scoop into the chocolate and pull it towards your body at a 45° angle until an even ice cream chocolate curl is formed. Repeat until most of the chocolate has been curled.

9. Scrape the leftover hardened chocolate from your worktop and remelt it. Use the shavings for decoration or set it aside for another time.

10. Repeat steps 3 – 9, using a different coloured chocolate each time, until all the melted chocolate has been used.

11. Put the ice cream chocolate scoops aside to cool completely.

12. Store in a dry, airtight container until you're ready to use it. The scoops/curls can be stored for up to one month.

Make the complete cake ★★

✓ Two square cakes (each 2 layers) of different sizes: 25 x 25 cm (10 x 10 in.) and 15 x 15 cm (6 x 6 in.)
✓ 1 square 30 cm (12 in.) cake board, plywood board, glass plate or cake stand
✓ 1 square 15 cm divider made from cardboard or foamalite, wrapped in aluminium foil or plastic cling wrap
✓ 3 batches of chocolate buttercream icing (recipe p. 141) or 3 batches each of dark chocolate ganache filling and coating (recipes p. 142 and p. 144)
✓ Chocolate ice cream scoops made with:
    800 g (1¾ lb) white chocolate
    10 ml (2 tsp) vegetable oil
    Food colouring, such as purple, blue, red and yellow
✓ Brightly coloured sweets such as Astros or Smarties

Assembling and decorating the cake

1. Fill and coat each cake with chocolate buttercream icing or dark chocolate ganache. (See instructions on p. 19: 'Filling and coating cakes'.)

2. Stack the cakes as per the instructions on p. 21.

3. Place chocolate ice cream scoops onto the top of all the cake tiers, lightly pushing them into the coating to adhere.

4. For an even brighter, flamboyant cake also add coloured sweets such as Smarties or Astros.

5. If you have not used a cake stand or serving plate, decorate your cake board, following the method on p. 22: 'Decorating a cake board'.

Mini cakes ★★

1. Remove the paper wrappers from your cupcakes and stick two cupcakes together with filling.

2. Cover with buttercream icing or ganache coating and push chocolate rolls into each mini cake.

Triangles

The hard and sharp edges of these triangles make this a masculine birthday cake for a boy or man.

Makes up to 20 servings.

Chocolate triangles ★★

These triangles are made in three different colours to add a quality of playfulness to the cake. Of course they can all be one colour, using the total amount of chocolate.

1. To make templates for the exact number of triangles you need to cover your cake:
   - Measure the height of the cake and add 2.5 cm (1 in.) to this measurement.
   - Measure the width of each of the three sides and add 10 cm (4 in.) to each of these measurements.
   - Cut three pieces of greaseproof paper to these new sizes so that you have one template for each side of the cake.

2. Now make a cutting template for the triangles: Using normal paper or light cardboard, cut a block the same height as the greaseproof paper and as wide as you want to make your largest triangles, for example 7.5 cm (3 in.) wide. Set aside to use later as a guide for cutting your chocolate into equal-sized panels.

3. Place one greaseproof paper template on a flat surface and use adhesive tape or masking tape to make a handle for each end and to keep the paper in place.

4. Melt 200 g (7 oz) dark or milk chocolate and pour onto the greaseproof paper in a thick line.

5. Quickly spread the chocolate with a palette knife from side to side and keep on spreading from one side to the other. Keep a 2.5 cm (1 in.) strip of paper open at each end by which you will later pick up the paper.

6. Spread the chocolate over the edges of the paper because the chocolate on the edges always sets more quickly than the chocolate in the middle. By keeping the chocolate moving, you regulate the temperature for the chocolate to set more evenly. Keep on spreading until the chocolate starts to thicken and set slightly. If you are working with eating chocolate only, this may take up to 30 minutes.

7. Touch the surface of the chocolate with your finger. If the chocolate starts to set but is still warm, with some chocolate coming off on your finger, the chocolate is ready to be lifted.

8. Quickly lift the paper off the work surface by holding the clean edges and lay it on a clean surface or on a baking or wooden tray that will fit into your refrigerator.

9. Wait for the chocolate to set and then place the cutting template on top of your chocolate. Using the outer edge of the template as a guide, cut through the chocolate with a knife or pizza wheel to make panels.

10. Using a ruler as a guide, cut each panel across diagonally to make triangles and also cut some of these triangles across diagonally to make smaller triangles (see photo).

11. After cutting all the triangles, place the tray containing the chocolate in the refrigerator for no longer than 10 minutes, to let the chocolate cool and set completely.

12. Scrape all leftover hardened chocolate from your worktop to use as decoration for the top of the cake.

13. To make the rest of the triangles, repeat steps 3 – 11, melting a batch of 200 g (7 oz) white chocolate for each template.
    – Colour one 200 g (7 oz) batch yellow by mixing 5 ml (1 tsp) vegetable oil with 30 drops of yellow liquid food colouring or 10 drops of paste food colouring.
    – Colour the other 200 g (7 oz) batch orange by mixing 5 ml (1 tsp) vegetable oil with 6 drops of red and 24 drops of yellow liquid food colouring or use 10 drops of paste food colouring.

14. Carefully remove the hardened chocolate triangles from the paper.

Tip

You will be making more triangles than you need to ensure that you have enough. Any leftover panels can be remelted and reused, e.g. for attaching the decorations to the cake.

Make the complete cake ★★

✓ 1 square single-layer 5 cm (2 in.) high cake of 25 x 25 cm (10 x 10 in.)
✓ 1 round 35 cm (14 in.) cake board or plywood board
✓ 1 batch of chocolate buttercream icing (recipe p. 141) or 1 batch each of dark chocolate ganache filling and coating (recipes p. 142 and p. 144)
✓ Chocolate triangles made with:
  200 g (7 oz) dark or milk chocolate
  400 g (14 oz) white chocolate
  10 ml (2 tsp) vegetable oil
  30 drops of yellow food colouring
  30 drops of orange food colouring
✓ 100 g (3½ oz) dark or milk chocolate melted, to attach decorations
✓ Small shavings made from leftover hardened chocolate
✓ Fresh berries, for example gooseberries, raspberries or grapes

Assembling and decorating the cake

1. Cut a large, equal-sided triangle from the square cake.

2. Fit the two leftover pieces together to form another, similar triangle.

3. Fill with buttercream icing or ganache filling and stack the two layers into a triangle of about 10 cm (4 in.) high.

4. Place on a cake board and coat the whole cake.

5. Pour the 100 g (3½ oz) melted dark or milk chocolate and into a Ziploc bag. Pipe chocolate on the back of each chocolate triangle before pressing it onto the cake.

6. Place the largest triangles against each other, overlapping where necessary, and stick smaller triangles on top of the bigger ones.

7. Spread a layer of the shavings you have saved from making the triangles on top of your cake.

8. Decorate the top with fresh berries.

9. If you have not used a cake stand or serving plate, decorate your cake board, following the method on p. 22: 'Decorating a cake board'.

Mini cakes ★★

1. Remove the paper wrappers from your cupcakes and stick two cupcakes together with filling.

2. Cover with buttercream icing or ganache coating.

3. Attach triangles to the sides with melted chocolate.

4. Decorate the top with chocolate shavings or fresh berries.

Individual cakes

These dainty little cakes with their decorative chocolate collars are large enough to share, although you won't want to!

Makes 1 to 2 servings per cake.

Make the complete cake ★★

Vary the cakes by changing the colour of the chocolate you use first and second. The instructions are given for one individual mini cake. It is easy to calculate quantities when you remember that for each individual cake you need:

- ✓ 2 cupcakes
- ✓ 60 ml (¼ cup) each ganache filling and coating (recipes p. 142 and p. 144)
- ✓ 30 g (1 oz) white chocolate, melted and coloured with 1.25 ml (¼ tsp) vegetable oil mixed with 2 drops of liquid food colouring
- ✓ 70 g (2½ oz) white or dark chocolate, melted
- ✓ Small cake board or plate made from cardboard covered with foil, slightly larger than the diameter of a cupcake, i.e. about 10 cm (4 in.)
- ✓ Chocolate shavings, truffles, fresh berries or flowers for decoration

Assembling and decorating the cakes

1. Remove the paper wrappers from the cupcakes.
2. Slice each cupcake into two layers, fill with ganache filling and stack the layers on top of one another.
3. Spread a teaspoon of ganache filling on a small cake board and place the mini cake on it.
4. Place the mini cake in the refrigerator for an hour, making it easier to cut.
5. Slice a sliver from the sides of the mini cake to make it even all round.
6. Cover with chocolate ganache coating.

7. Make a template for the chocolate collar:
   - Measure the mini cake's height and add 2.5 cm (1 in.) to this measurement.
   - Measure the circumference of the mini cake and add 2.5 cm (1 in.) to this measurement.
   - Cut a piece of greaseproof paper to this new size.

8. Place the paper template on a flat surface, using adhesive tape or masking tape to make a handle for each end and to keep the paper in place.

9. Melt and colour 30 g (1 oz) white chocolate, pour into a Ziploc bag and snip off a corner to make a piping bag.

10. Pipe the coloured chocolate over the paper in any pattern you prefer. Wait until the chocolate sets slightly otherwise it will smudge.

11. Melt 70 g (2½ oz) white or dark chocolate and pour in a thick line onto the paper, over your design.

12. Quickly spread the chocolate with a palette knife from side to side and keep on spreading from one side to the other. Keep the chocolate moving to regulate the temperature and help the chocolate set evenly. With these small collars extend only slightly over the edges of the paper. Keep on spreading until the chocolate starts to thicken and set slightly.

13. Touch the surface of the chocolate with your finger. If the chocolate is slightly firm but still warm, with some chocolate coming off onto your finger, the collar is ready to be lifted.

14. Quickly lift the paper off the work surface by holding onto the adhesive tape at both ends and lifting it. Press the chocolate side onto the mini cake, with the paper on the outside.

15. Use your hands to guide the paper to form a cylindrical shape. Pull off the adhesive tape and fold one edge over the other.

16. Place the mini cake in the refrigerator for no longer than 10 minutes, just to let the chocolate set completely.

17. Remove the cake from the refrigerator and carefully remove the paper. Where the ends of the paper meet, slowly wriggle out the paper from under the top chocolate seam.

18. Scrape all leftover hardened chocolate from your worktop and reuse once for another cake or for making ganache.

19. Add more filling and decorations to the top of the small cake.

Tip

Keep the melted chocolate warm on a hot tray set at its lowest setting, on top of a folded dish cloth or periodically reheat the chocolate in the microwave oven at 50% power for 10 seconds at a time when the chocolate starts to set on the side of the bowl.

Polka panels

Polka dots are lots of fun. This cake can be made for any gender and is especially popular for 21st birthdays and anniversaries. Dress it up even more by adding chocolate daisies.

Makes up to 36 servings.

Chocolate panels ★★

Keeping in mind that 100 g (3½ oz) of chocolate will make three panels, you can work out exactly how many panels and how much chocolate you will need to cover your cake. The amounts given in the instructions are for the illustrated cake.

1. Make a template for creating the exact number of panels you need:
   - Measure the height of the cake and add 2.5 cm (1 in.) to this measurement.
   - Measure the circumference of the cake and add 10 cm (4 in.) to this measurement.
   - Cut a piece of greaseproof paper to this new size. If the paper is too long to fit onto a tray that will go into your refrigerator, cut it in half and make two separate pieces.

2. Place the paper on a flat surface and use adhesive tape or masking tape to make a handle for each end and to keep the paper in place.

3. Now make a cutting template for the chocolate panels: Using normal paper or light cardboard, cut a block of paper the same height as the greaseproof paper and as wide as you want to make your panels, for example approximately 12.5 cm (5 in.) high and 7.5 cm (3 in.) wide. Set aside to use later.

4. Melt 50 g (2 oz) white chocolate and colour it with 1.25 ml (¼ tsp) vegetable oil mixed with up to 7 drops of yellow food colouring. Pour into a Ziploc bag.

5. Melt another 50 g (2 oz) white chocolate and pour into a Ziploc bag.

6. Snip off a corner of each Ziploc bag to make piping bags and pipe dots of coloured and white chocolate onto the paper, varying the sizes or keeping them all the same size if you prefer. Wait until the chocolate sets slightly, otherwise it will smudge.

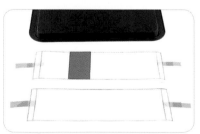

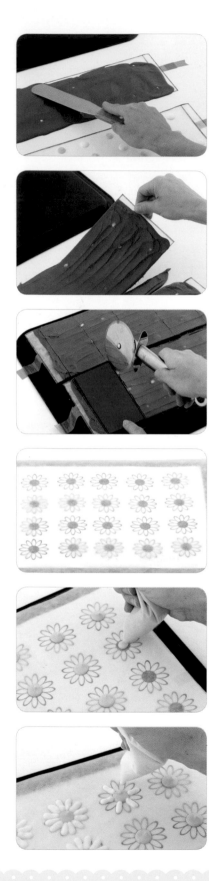

7. Melt 675 g (1½ lb) dark or milk chocolate and pour in a thick line onto the paper(s) over your polka dots.

8. Quickly spread the chocolate with a palette knife and keep on spreading from one side to the other. Keep a 2.5 cm (1 in.) strip of paper open at each end by which you will later pick up the template. Spread the chocolate slightly over the top edges of the paper because the chocolate on the edges always sets more quickly than the chocolate in the middle. By keeping the chocolate moving, you regulate the temperature for the chocolate to set more evenly. Keep on spreading until the chocolate starts to thicken and set slightly. If using only eating chocolate, this may take up to 30 minutes.

9. Touch the surface of the chocolate with your finger. If the chocolate is slightly firm but still warm, with some chocolate coming off onto your finger, the chocolate is ready to be lifted.

10. Quickly lift the paper off the work surface by holding the clean strips and adhesive tape at both ends, and lay it on a clean surface or on a baking or wooden tray that will fit into your refrigerator.

11. Place the cutting template on top of your chocolate and, using the edges as a guide, cut through the chocolate with a knife or pizza wheel to make your panels.

12. After cutting all the blocks, place the tray with chocolate panels in the refrigerator for no longer than 10 minutes, just to let the chocolate cool and set completely.

13. Remove the chocolate polka-dot panels from the refrigerator and carefully peel them from the paper.

Chocolate daisies ★

At the back of this book are templates for daisies (see p. 158). Copy the design a few times on paper that will fit on a baking tin (sheet) or wooden tray. To make up to 30 daisies, use 150 g (5 oz) white chocolate.

1. Lay the paper with the daisy designs in a baking or wooden tray that will fit into your refrigerator.

2. Cut greaseproof paper to place over the daisy template and secure the paper onto the tray with adhesive tape. If working with eating chocolate only, you can place the tray in the refrigerator for 20 minutes before making your decorations on it.

3. Melt 50 g (2 oz) white chocolate and colour it with 1.25 ml (¼ tsp) vegetable oil mixed with up to 7 drops of yellow food colouring.

4. Pour into a Ziploc bag and snip off a corner to make a piping bag.

5. Pipe dots of coloured chocolate onto the paper to make the daisy centres, leaving enough space between the dots to pipe the daisy petals.

6. Melt another 100 g (3½ oz) white chocolate and pour into a Ziploc bag. Snip off a corner of the Ziploc bag to make a piping bag.

7. Pipe long cone shapes with the white chocolate to form the daisy petals.

8. Put the tray with the daisies into the refrigerator for no longer than 10 minutes.

9. Take the tray out of the refrigerator and carefully lift the daisies off the paper.

10. If you want some of the daisies to stand upright in your cake, remelt some leftover chocolate in your Ziploc piping bags in the microwave oven. Pipe a little chocolate onto the back of some of the daisies, stick a toothpick into this dot of chocolate and pipe a little more over the toothpick to secure it.

11. Repeat the steps with the remaining chocolate until you have enough.

Make the complete cake

- ✓ 1 round cake (2 layers) of 25 cm (10 in.)
- ✓ 1 round 35 cm (14 in.) cake board, plywood board or cake stand
- ✓ 1½ batch of chocolate buttercream icing (recipe p. 141) or 1½ batch each of dark chocolate ganache filling and coating (recipes p. 142 and p. 144)
- ✓ Chocolate panels made with:
      100 g (3½ oz) white chocolate
      1.25 ml (¼ tsp) vegetable oil
      7 drops of yellow food colouring
      675 g (1½ lb) dark or milk chocolate
- ✓ Chocolate daisies made with:
      150 g (5 oz) white chocolate
      1.25 ml (¼ tsp) vegetable oil
      7 drops of yellow food colouring
      100 g (3½ oz) dark or milk chocolate melted, to attach decorations

Assembling and decorating the cake

1. Divide the layers and fill with chocolate buttercream icing or dark chocolate ganache filling. (See instructions on p. 19: 'Filling and coating cakes'.)

2. Place on a cake board and coat the cake with buttercream or ganache.

3. Spread or pipe the 100 g (3½ oz) melted dark or milk chocolate on the back of each panel before pressing the panels onto the cake.

4. Add daisies to the top of the cake.

5. If you have not used a cake stand or serving plate, decorate your cake board, following the method on p. 22: 'Decorating a cake board'.

Cupcakes

Spread the top of your cupcakes with buttercream icing or chocolate ganache coating and place a chocolate daisy on top of each cupcake.

Candy-stripe curved collar

Why not surprise your mother on her birthday or Mother's Day with this purple striped cake? It is quite a feminine cake that any woman would adore. If you do not have time to make chocolate paste roses, just use fresh roses instead.

Makes up to 24 servings.

Candy-stripe curved collar ★★

1. Make a template for the exact size of collar you need to cover your cake:
   - Measure the height of the cake and add 2.5 cm (1 in.) to this measurement.
   - Measure the circumference of the cake and add 5 cm (2 in.) to this measurement.
   - Cut a piece of greaseproof paper to this size.
2. Draw a wave pattern on the top edge of the paper and cut it out with scissors or use 'scrapbook' scissors to cut a pattern.
3. Place the paper on a flat surface and use adhesive tape or masking tape to make a handle for each end and to keep the paper in place.
4. Melt 100 g (3½ oz) white chocolate and colour it according to your colour scheme (for example purple: 2.5 ml (½ tsp) vegetable oil mixed with 8 drops of blue food colouring and 2 drops of red food colouring or 2 drops of violet paste food colouring).
5. Pour the melted, coloured chocolate into a Ziploc bag and snip off a corner to make a piping bag.
6. Pipe the coloured chocolate over the paper in any pattern you prefer. If you want straight lines, use a ruler as guide. Wait until the chocolate sets slightly, otherwise it will smudge.
7. Melt 450 g (1 lb) dark chocolate and pour in a thick line onto the paper over your design.
8. Quickly spread the chocolate with a palette knife and keep on spreading from one side to the other. Keep a 2.5 cm (1 in.) strip of paper open at one end by which you will later pick up the collar. Spread the chocolate over the edges of the paper because the chocolate on the edges always sets more quickly than the chocolate in the middle. By keeping the chocolate moving, you regulate the temperature for the chocolate to set more evenly. Keep on spreading until the chocolate starts to thicken and set slightly. If using only eating chocolate, this may take up to 30 minutes.

9. Touch the surface of the chocolate with your finger. If the chocolate is slightly firm but still warm, with some chocolate coming off onto your finger, the collar is ready to be lifted.

10. Quickly lift the paper off the work surface by holding the clean paper at one end and the adhesive tape at the other, and press the collar onto the cake with the chocolate side against the cake and the paper on the outside.

11. With your hands, guide the paper all the way around the cake and fold the edges one over the other.

12. Put the cake in the refrigerator for no longer than 10 minutes, to let the chocolate cool and set completely.

13. Scrape all leftover hardened chocolate from your countertop to reuse once for another cake or for making ganache filling.

14. After the fitted collar has set, carefully remove the paper. Where the ends of the paper meet, slowly wriggle out the paper from under the top chocolate seam.

15. With a sharp knife or pizza wheel, carefully cut off the overlapping chocolate seam so that the two ends meet neatly.

16. Dab some melted chocolate on the inside of the collar where the seam meets, to seal the join.

Chocolate paste roses and leaves ★★

The quantity described here will give you 15 five-petalled roses and 15 leaves.

1. Make a double quantity of white chocolate paste (see recipe on p. 148), using 600 g (1¼ lb) white chocolate, 125 ml (4½ fl oz/½ cup) golden syrup or glucose syrup and 20 ml (1 tbsp & 1 tsp) water.

2. Divide the paste, using ±700 g (1½ lb) for the roses and ±100 g (3½ oz) for the leaves.

3. Colour the larger quantity of paste according to your colour scheme with food colouring, for example purple (mix blue and red food colouring if you don't have purple).

4. Colour the smaller quantity with a few drops of green food colouring until you have your desired shade and place in the refrigerator until needed.

5. Use icing sugar (confectioner's sugar) to dust your hands if the paste feels sticky. Using latex gloves will protect your hands from getting stained and will also prevent the paste from sticking while you are kneading it.

6. To form the centres of the roses, take 150 g (5 oz) of the purple paste and roll 15 evenly-sized balls.

7. Roll each ball into a sausage and then flatten each sausage with a rolling pin or glass bottle on greaseproof paper or inside a plastic bag.

8. Roll up each sausage of paste to form the centre and place in the refrigerator until needed.

9. To form the rose petals, divide the rest of the purple paste into 75 even-sized balls of about 7 g (¼ oz) each to make 5 petals per rose.

10. Flatten each ball by pinching it between your fingers or by placing it on greaseproof paper or inside a plastic bag and rolling over the paste with a rolling pin or glass bottle.

11. If the paste becomes too soft, place in the refrigerator for 5 minutes to harden slightly.

12. To make life-like petals, pinch the top edges between your fingers to flatten and thin them. Pinch an indent in the middle of each petal to resemble a rose petal.

13. Wrap the petal around the centre of your rose, slightly curling the top edge open. If it doesn't stick, use a few drops of cooled boiled water to act as glue.

14. Attach a second petal to the centre, opposite the first one, also slightly curling the petal open. Try to tuck the petals underneath each other to look more realistic.

15. Attach three more petals in the same way.

16. Set the roses aside to dry or store the roses, covered in cling wrap, in the refrigerator until you're ready to use them.

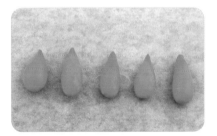
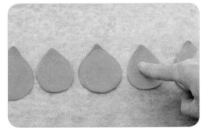
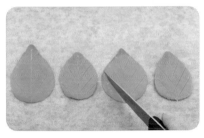

17. To make the leaves, use the green chocolate paste and roll 15 evenly-sized balls of about 7 g (¼ oz) each between your hands. Roll each ball into a cone shape.

18. Flatten each cone on a piece of greaseproof paper or inside a plastic bag by pressing with your fingers onto the paste or rolling over the paste with a rolling pin or glass bottle until it looks like a leaf.

19. Make leaf markings on the flattened pieces with a knife.

20. Place crumpled foil on a baking tray and arrange the leaves on this. When they dry, they will look more life-like.

21. Store the leaves, covered in cling wrap, in the refrigerator until you're ready to use them.

Tip

The roses and leaves can be made up to two weeks ahead and stored in an airtight container in a cool, dark cupboard.

Make the complete cake ★★

✓ 1 round cake (2 layers) of 20 cm (8 in.)
✓ 1 round 30 cm (12 in.) cake board, plywood board, serving plate or a cake stand
✓ 1 batch of chocolate buttercream icing (recipe p. 141) or 1 batch each of dark chocolate ganache filling and coating (recipes p. 142 and p. 144)
✓ Candy-stripe curved collar made with:
    100 g (3½ oz) white chocolate
    2.5 ml (½ tsp) vegetable oil
    10 drops purple food colouring or 2 drops of violet paste food colouring
    450 g (1 lb) dark chocolate
✓ 15 chocolate paste roses and 15 leaves made with:
    600 g (1 lb 6 oz) white chocolate,
    125 ml (4½ fl oz/½ cup) golden syrup or glucose syrup
    20 ml (1 tbsp & 1 tsp) water
    Food colouring such as purple and green

Assembling and decorating the cake

1. Divide and fill the layers with buttercream icing or ganache filling. (See instructions on p. 19: 'Filling and coating cakes'.)

2. Stack the layers on a cake board and coat the cake.

3. Make and fit the candy-stripe collar as described.

4. Make the chocolate paste roses and leaves as described and add to the top of your cake.

5. As an alternative to paste roses, decorate the cake with fresh flowers.

6. If you have not used a cake stand or serving plate, decorate your cake board, following the method on p. 22: 'Decorating a cake board'.

Mini cakes ★★

1. Remove the paper wrappers from your cupcakes and stick two cupcakes together with filling.

2. Place the mini cakes in the refrigerator for an hour, making them easier to cut.

3. Slice a sliver from all sides to make the mini cakes even all round.

4. Cover with buttercream icing or ganache coating.

5. Take the measurements of one mini cake and use that to make templates for all of them.

6. Make chocolate collars as described on p. 81: 'Individual cakes'.

7. Place a chocolate paste rose and leaf on top of each mini cake.

Funky rolls and shavings

Everybody loves cupcakes, the perfectly-sized individual cakes for a celebration. You can make them for a child's birthday party or an adult's alike.

Makes 24 servings.

Funky rolls ★★

- These colourful rolls and shavings are enough for 24 cupcakes. Make them in the colours of your choice.
- The amount of chocolate used in this recipe is 200 g (7 oz) white and 200 g (7 oz) dark chocolate.
- To adjust the amount, remember that 100 g (3½ oz) chocolate makes ±15 rolls and some shavings.

1. You will need to melt four batches of white chocolate, each consisting of 50 g (2 oz), and colour each batch separately with 1.25 ml (¼ tsp) vegetable oil mixed with 5 drops of liquid food colouring, e.g. green, red or pink, blue and yellow, to give you four different colours.
2. You will also need to melt 200 g (7 oz) dark chocolate, which is divided into four batches, for use with each different colour.
3. Have your 50 g (2 oz) coloured chocolate and 50 g (2 oz) dark chocolate melted and ready to use at the same time.
4. Start with any colour of chocolate: pour the chocolate onto your work surface (a marble slab, flat tile, thick rectangular glass plate, stainless steel or granite counter). If the marble slab or tile becomes too hot and the chocolate doesn't set as quickly, refrigerate it until it feels cooler. If using a stainless steel or granite counter, use different parts of the countertop to pour the chocolate onto so that one part doesn't become too heated.
5. Spread the coloured chocolate with a dough or metal scraper or palette knife until it cools slightly and becomes thicker. Then spread it flat into a thin layer.
6. Using a comb with wide-set teeth or a large fork, scrape even grooves in the flat layer of coloured chocolate.
7. While you are waiting for the chocolate to set, clean the excess chocolate off the scraper or palette knife with a sharp knife and set aside to remelt or for use in another project.

8. Pour the 50 g (2 oz) melted dark chocolate onto the first coloured chocolate and spread it very lightly over the flat layer.

9. Let the chocolate set. This will take a few seconds only. Press your finger onto the chocolate and if it still feels slightly warm but does not leave a fingerprint, it is ready to use.

10. Use an ice cream scoop to form the rolls. Push the scoop into the chocolate and pull it towards your body at a 45° angle until an even roll is formed. Repeat until most of the chocolate has been rolled.

11. Scrape the leftover hardened chocolate from your counter top to use as shavings and set aside.

12. Repeat the above steps with each of the different colours.

13. Put the rolls and shavings aside to cool completely.

14. Store the rolls and shavings separately in dry, airtight containers until needed. They can be stored for up to one month.

Make the complete cake ★

✓ *24 cupcakes*
✓ *Buttercream icing or ganache coating*
✓ *Special cupcake wrappers. You can buy these or make your own from light cardboard, using the template on p. 158*
✓ *Funky rolls and shavings made from:*
      200 g (7 oz) white chocolate
      5 ml (1 tsp) vegetable oil
      20 drops of liquid food colouring, e.g. green, red or pink, blue and yellow
      200 g (7 oz) dark chocolate

Assembling and decorating the cupcakes

1. Ice the tops of the cupcakes with buttercream icing or ganache coating.

2. Place each cupcake inside a special cupcake wrapper if you prefer.

3. Decorate 12 of the cupcakes with the finished rolls. Use 4 – 5 rolls per cupcake.

4. Decorate the other 12 cupcakes with shavings. Use ±15 ml (1 tbsp) per cupcake.

Square polka dot cake

Crisply neat dots do the polka on this festive cake.

Makes up to 40 servings.

Cut-out chocolate polka dots ★

These polka dots are made with assorted round metal cutters.

1. Melt three batches of white chocolate:
   - 100 g (3½ oz) coloured with 2.5 ml (½ tsp) vegetable oil mixed with 10 drops of liquid food colouring or 2 or more drops of paste food colouring of your choice, e.g. green.
   - A second batch of 100 g (3½ oz) coloured with 2.5 ml (½ tsp) vegetable oil mixed with 10 drops of liquid food colouring or 2 or more drops of paste food colouring of your choice, e.g. blue.
   - A smaller batch of 50 g (2 oz) coloured with 1.25 ml (¼ tsp) vegetable oil mixed with 5 drops of liquid food colouring or a drop or two of paste food colouring, e.g. yellow.

2. Cut three pieces of greaseproof paper to line a baking tin (sheet) or wooden tray that will fit into your refrigerator. Using one piece of paper at a time, secure the paper by sticking it to the tray with adhesive tape or masking tape. If working with eating chocolate only, place the tray in the refrigerator for 20 minutes before making your decorations on it.

3. Start with one colour chocolate. Pour the melted, coloured chocolate into your prepared tray and quickly spread the chocolate with a palette knife from side to side and keep on spreading from one side to the other. By keeping the chocolate moving, you regulate the temperature and therefore the chocolate sets more evenly.

4. Keep on spreading until the chocolate starts to thicken and set slightly. If you are using eating chocolate, this will take quite a while so, to speed up the process, you can put the tray in the refrigerator for 5 minutes at a time and keep on spreading the chocolate from side to side until set.

5. Touch the surface of the chocolate with your finger. If the chocolate feels firm, without chocolate coming off onto your finger, it is ready to be cut into polka dots.

6. Use different-sized round metal cutters to cut polka dots, also cutting a smaller circle into some of the larger circles.

7. Place the tray in the refrigerator for 10 minutes for the chocolate to set.

8. Remove the tray and pull the cut-out polka dots from the paper. Turn the polka dots over and use the flat side as the front.

9. Dip toothpicks into some of the remelted chocolate and place onto the backs of a few polka dots. When the chocolate has set, these can be used on top of the cake as stand-up polka dots.

10. Repeat the steps with the other two colours of chocolate.

11. The cut-out polka dots can be stored in an airtight container in a cool, dark cupboard for up to two weeks.

Make the complete cake ★

✓ 1 square cake (2 layers) of 20 x 20 cm (8 x 8 in.)
✓ 1 square 30 cm (12 in.) cake board, plywood board, serving plate or cake stand
✓ 1¼ batch of chocolate buttercream icing (recipe p. 141) or 1¼ batch each dark chocolate ganache filling and coating (recipes p. 142 and p. 144)
✓ Chocolate cut-out polka dots made with:
    250 g (9 oz) white chocolate
    6.25 ml (1 ¼ tsp) vegetable oil
    25 drops of liquid food colouring eg. blue, green and yellow
✓ 100 g (3½ oz) dark chocolate melted, to attach the decorations

Assembling and decorating the cake

1. Divide and fill the layers and coat the whole cake with chocolate buttercream or dark chocolate ganache. (See instructions on p. 19: 'Filling and coating cakes'.)

2. Pour the 100 g (3½ oz) melted dark chocolate into a Ziploc bag and snip off a corner to make a piping bag.

3. Decorate the cake by piping some melted chocolate onto the back of each polka dot and pressing it onto the cake. Start at the top of the cake and work towards the bottom.

4. Push some of the polka dots on toothpicks into the top of the cake.

5. Follow the method on p. 22: 'Decorating a cake board'.

Mini cakes ★

1. Use any rectangular cake cut into squares.

2. Cover your mini cakes with chocolate buttercream icing or dark chocolate ganache coating.

3. Dab melted chocolate onto the backs of the polka dots and press onto the sides of the mini cakes.

4. Decorate the tops with polka dots on toothpicks.

Cigarillos and truffles

Cigarillos look like small cigars but have the exquisite taste of chocolate. Each person gets a piece of cake with their own chocolates to savour.

Makes up to 100 servings.

Chocolate cigarillos ★★★

- Cigarillos or rolls in the natural shades of chocolate and even marbled!
- The cake demonstrated in this project needs about 200 cigarillos, which seems like a lot, but once you master the skill of making rolls, you will find it great fun!
- If you would like to make fewer cigarillos for a smaller cake, use the following guideline: 450 g (1 lb) of chocolate makes approximately 45 cigarillos or rolls weighing about 10 g (⅓ oz) each.

White rolls

1. Melt 600 g (1¼ lb) white chocolate. Pour about 250 ml (9 fl oz/1 cup) of the melted chocolate onto a marble slab, flat tile, thick rectangular glass plate, stainless steel counter or granite worktop. (If the marble slab, tile or glass plate becomes too hot and the chocolate doesn't set quickly enough, refrigerate it until it feels cooler. If using a stainless steel or granite worktop, use different parts of the worktop to pour the chocolate onto so that one part doesn't become too heated.)
2. Spread the chocolate from side to side with a dough or metal scraper or palette knife until it cools slightly and becomes thicker.
3. When the chocolate starts to set, spread it flat into a thin layer.
4. While waiting for the chocolate to cool and set, clean the excess chocolate.
5. Press your finger onto the chocolate and if it still feels slightly warm but does not leave a fingerprint, it is ready to use.

6. To form even rolls, push the scraper into the flat chocolate, away from your body, at a 45° angle until an even chocolate roll is formed.
7. Or, if you want to form uneven rolls, use a sharp knife instead of a scraper and pull the chocolate towards you at a 45° angle.
8. If any chocolate sticks to your scraper or knife, scrape it off.
9. Scrape the leftover hardened chocolate from your worktop and remelt for more rolls.

10. Repeat these steps with the rest of the white chocolate until all the chocolate has been used. You will need to make 50 – 60 rolls.

11. Put all the rolls aside to cool completely.

12. Store the rolls in a dry, airtight container until you're ready to use them. The rolls can be stored for up to one month.

Dark rolls

1. Melt 1 kg (2 lb) dark chocolate and make rolls using exactly the same steps as in making white rolls.

2. Repeat the steps until all the dark chocolate has been used. You will need to make 90 – 100 rolls.

Marbled rolls

1. Melt 700 g (1½ lb) white chocolate and 100 g (3½ oz) dark chocolate separately.

2. Pour about 250 ml (9 fl oz/1 cup) of the melted white chocolate onto your worktop and follow steps 1 – 2 for making white rolls, to a point where the white chocolate has cooled and thickened slightly.

3. To create the marbling effect, pour 15 ml (1 tbsp) of dark chocolate over the white chocolate and spread the two chocolate colours into each other to mix. Do not overmix: the chocolate must be only slightly marbled.

4. Now proceed with the rest of the steps as in making white rolls, repeating these steps with the rest of the white and dark chocolate until all the chocolate has been used. Remelt the hardened, scraped-off, marbled chocolate to make more rolls. You will need to make 70 – 80 rolls.

Mini cakes ★★

1. Remove the paper wrappers from your cupcakes and stick two cupcakes together with filling.

2. Place the mini cakes in the refrigerator for an hour, making them easier to cut.

3. Slice a sliver from all sides to make the mini cakes even all round.

4. Cover with buttercream icing or ganache coating.

5. Use melted chocolate to stick cigarillos around each mini cake.

6. Place a chocolate truffle or flower on top of each mini cake.

Note: The three-tiered cake in this project is about 30 cm (12 in.) high. If your cake is smaller, decrease the amounts of buttercream icing, ganache and chocolate needed.

Make the complete cake ★★★

✓ *3 round cakes (each 2 layers) of different sizes: 25 cm (10 in.), 20 cm (8 in.) and 15 cm (6 in.)*

✓ *1 round 35 cm (14 in.) cake board, plywood board, serving plate or cake stand*

✓ *2 round dividers made from cardboard or foamalite, wrapped in aluminium foil or plastic cling wrap in different sizes: 20 cm (8 in.) and 15 cm (6 in.)*

✓ *1½ batch of plain buttercream icing (recipe p. 140) or 1½ batch each of white chocolate ganache filling and coating (recipes p. 142 and p. 144) for the top two tiers*

✓ *1 batch of chocolate buttercream icing or 1 batch each of dark chocolate ganache filling and coating for the bottom tier*

✓ *50 – 60 white chocolate cigarillos made with 600 g (1¼ lb) white chocolate for the 15 cm (6 in.) cake*

✓ *70 – 80 marbled chocolate cigarillos made with 700 g (1½ lb) white chocolate and 100 g (3½ oz) dark chocolate*

✓ *90 – 100 dark chocolate cigarillos made with 1 kg (2 lb) dark chocolate for the 25 cm (10 in.) cake*

✓ *40 white and dark chocolate truffles*

✓ *6 – 12 fresh flowers, such as roses or gerberas*

Assembling and decorating the cake

1. For the top two tiers, divide and fill each layer and coat the cakes with a thin layer of plain buttercream icing or white chocolate ganache (see instructions on p. 19: 'Filling and coating cakes'). For the bottom tier, use a thin layer of chocolate buttercream icing or dark chocolate ganache for filling and coating.

2. Stack the tiers with the largest placed on the cake board and the others on their dividers. (See the method for stacking tiers on p. 21.)

3. Scrape the leftover buttercream or ganache into a big Ziploc bag and decorate the cake by piping lines up and down the cake.

4. Press the cigarillos into the icing or coating, using the white rolls on the top cake, the marbled rolls on the middle cake and the dark rolls on the bottom cake.

5. Arrange the truffles on the cake.

6. Push a toothpick into the stem of each flower and push the toothpick into the cake.

7. Decorate your cake board, following the method on p. 22: 'Decorating a cake board'.

Full lace collar

This delicately light lace design works well for a feminine birthday cake, a bridal shower or even a wedding cake.

Makes up to 100 servings.

Full lace collar ★★

Each tier of the cake is decorated with its own lace collar. Make and fit the collar for the smallest, top tier first, then the middle, and lastly the bottom tier.

1. Make templates for each of the three collars by measuring the height and circumference of each tier.

2. Add 2.5 cm (1 in.) to each height measurement and 5 cm (2 in.) to each circumference measurement. Cut three pieces of greaseproof paper to these new measurements.

3. Place the smallest template on a flat surface, using adhesive tape or masking tape to make a handle for each end and to keep the paper in place.

4. Melt 300 g (10½ oz) dark chocolate. Pour one ¼ or about 80 g (3 oz) of the chocolate into a Ziploc bag and snip off a corner to make a piping bag.

5. Pipe the chocolate over the paper by swirling the chocolate in circles in a lace pattern. Keep 2.5 cm (1 in.) of the paper open on one side for lifting the collar off the work surface.

6. If the chocolate sets too quickly, blow hot air over the chocolate with a hair-dryer to remelt it slightly. If the chocolate is slightly firm but still warm, with some chocolate coming off onto your finger, the collar is ready to be lifted.

7. Quickly lift the paper off the work surface by holding the clean strip at one end and the adhesive tape at the other end. Press the collar onto the cake with the chocolate side against the cake and the paper on the outside.

8. Use your hands to guide the paper all the way around the cake and fold one edge over the other.

9. Place the cake with the collar in the refrigerator for 10 minutes.

10. When the fitted collar has set, carefully remove the paper. Where the ends of the paper meet, slowly wriggle out the paper from under the top choco-late seam.

11. Make the other two collars in the same way, starting with the middle tier. Use about 100 g (3½ oz) of the melted chocolate for the middle tier and the rest of the chocolate, about 120 g (4 oz), for the bottom tier.

Make the complete cake ★★★

- ✓ 3 round cakes (each 2 layers) of different sizes: 25 cm (10 in.), 20 cm (8 in.) and 15 cm (6 in.)
- ✓ 1 round 35 cm (14 in.) cake board, plywood board, serving plate or cake stand
- ✓ 2 round dividers made from cardboard or foamalite, wrapped in aluminium foil or plastic cling wrap in different sizes: 20 cm (8 in.) and 15 cm (6 in.)
- ✓ 3 batches of chocolate buttercream icing (recipe p. 141) or 3 batches each of dark chocolate ganache filling and coating (recipes p. 142 and p. 144)
- ✓ Lace collars made with 300 g (10½ oz) dark chocolate
- ✓ 3 – 6 fresh flowers, e.g. lilies or stargazers

Assembling and decorating the cake

1. Divide and fill each layer with buttercream icing or ganache filling. (See instructions on p. 19: 'Filling and coating cakes'.)
2. Coat each cake and stack the tiers by following the method on p. 21.
3. Make and fit the lace collars for each tier, starting with the smallest one.
4. Decorate your cake board, following the method on p. 22: 'Decorating a cake board' and place fresh flowers on the cake.

Tip

Reuse Ziploc bags by washing them in hot soapy water. Let them dry completely before reusing.

Mini cakes ★★

1. Remove the paper wrappers from your cupcakes and stick two cupcakes together with filling.
2. Place the mini cakes in the refrigerator for an hour, making them easier to cut.
3. Slice a sliver from all sides to make the mini cakes even all round.
4. Cover with buttercream icing or ganache coating.
5. Take the measurements of one mini cake and use that to make templates for all of them.
6. Make a chocolate lace collar for each mini cake.
7. Decorate with a chocolate truffle, shavings or a fresh flower.

Light and dark stripes

This retro-inspired cake would be ideal for a modern wedding.

Makes up to 80 servings.

Light and dark stripes ★★

These stripes can be placed in an orderly or haphazard fashion but will always make an impression. Amounts given here are for a very large cake. Adjust for a smaller cake.

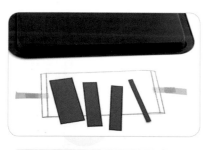

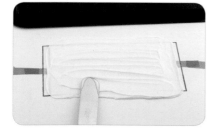

1. Make templates for each tier of the cake by measuring the height and width of one side of the top tier as well as of the bottom tier.

2. Add 2.5 cm (1 in.) to each of the height measurements and 10 cm (4 in.) to each of the width measurements.

3. Cut four pieces of greaseproof paper to the new measurement of the top tier, as well as four pieces for the bottom tier. For each tier, two pieces of paper will be used to make dark stripes and two pieces will be used to make light stripes.

4. Make different cutting templates for the chocolate out of normal paper or light cardboard by cutting blocks of the same height as the greaseproof paper templates and as wide as you want to make your stripes, e.g. 1.25 cm (½ in.), 2.5 cm (1 in.) and 5 cm (2 in.) wide. Set aside to use later as guides for cutting your chocolate.

5. Starting with the greaseproof paper templates for the smaller top tier, place one template at a time on a flat surface, using adhesive tape or masking tape to make a handle for each end and to keep the paper in place.

6. Melt 600 g (1¼ lb) white chocolate.

7. Pour about 250 ml (9 fl oz/1 cup) of the melted white chocolate onto the paper in a thick line.

8. Quickly spread the chocolate with a palette knife from side to side and keep on spreading from one side to the other, keeping a 2.5 cm (1 in.) strip of paper open at each end. Spread the chocolate slightly over the edges of the paper because the chocolate on the edges always sets more quickly than the chocolate in the middle. By keeping the chocolate moving, you regulate the temperature for the chocolate to set more evenly. Keep on spreading until the chocolate starts to thicken and set slightly.

9. Touch the surface of the chocolate with your finger. If the chocolate is slightly firm but still warm, with some chocolate coming off onto your finger the paper is ready to be lifted.

10. Quickly lift the paper off the work surface by holding the clean edges and adhesive tape and lay it on a baking or wooden tray that will fit into your refrigerator.

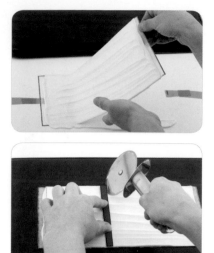

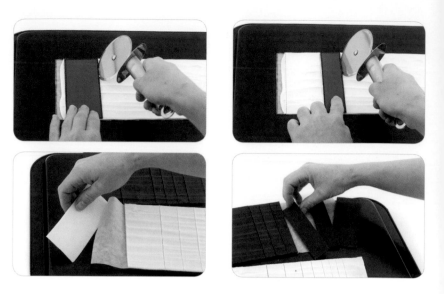

Tip

Taking measurements and using templates mean less chocolate wasted and total control over the size of your decorations. When you start marketing your beautifully decorated cakes and have to calculate the costs involved, you will find these guidelines invaluable.

11. Wait for the chocolate to set and then place the cutting templates on top of your chocolate. Using the outer edges of the templates as a guide, cut through the chocolate with a knife or pizza wheel to make stripes. Remember that you want the stripes to stand slightly higher than the tiers.

12. Place the tray with the chocolate in the refrigerator for no longer than 10 minutes, just to let the chocolate cool and set completely.

13. Scrape all leftover hardened chocolate from your countertop into a clean bowl to remelt.

14. Remove the chocolate stripes from the refrigerator and carefully remove them from the paper.

15. Repeat all the steps with the white chocolate, using a second greaseproof paper template for the top tier and two of the greaseproof paper templates for the bottom tier.

16. Melt 600 g (1¼ lb) dark chocolate. To make it even darker, you can colour the chocolate by adding 10 ml (2 tsp) vegetable oil mixed with 2.5 ml (½ tsp) liquid food colouring (mix together all your darkest to make black) or 5 ml (1 tsp) black powder colouring or 1.25 ml (¼ tsp) black paste food colouring.

17. Repeat all the steps until you have two greaseproof paper templates with dark or black chocolate stripes for the top and two for the bottom tier.

Mini cakes ★★

1. Bake a rectangular sheet cake and cut it into squares.

2. Cover your cakes with buttercream icing or ganache coating.

3. Spread melted chocolate on the back of each stripe and push it onto the sides of the mini cakes. Decorate them with fresh flowers or berries.

Make the complete cake ★★★

- ✓ 2 square cakes (each 2 layers) of 25 x 25 cm (10 x 10 in.) and 15 x 15 cm (6 x 6 in.)
- ✓ 1 square 35 x 35 cm (14 x 14 in.) cake board or plywood board
- ✓ 1 square 15 x 15 cm (6 x 6 in.) divider made from thick cardboard or foamalite, wrapped in aluminium foil or plastic cling wrap
- ✓ 3 batches of plain or chocolate buttercream icing (recipe p. 141) or 3 batches each of white or dark chocolate ganache filling and coating (recipes p. 142 and p. 144)
- ✓ Light and dark stripes made with:
  - 600 g (1¼ lb) dark chocolate
  - 10 ml (2 tsp) vegetable oil
  - Food colouring such as black
  - 600 g (1¼ lb) white chocolate
- ✓ 100 g (3 ½ oz) dark or white chocolate melted, to attach stripes
- ✓ 30 – 40 fresh red roses or 450 g (1 lb) fresh red berries, e.g. strawberries and raspberries

Assembling and decorating the cake

1. Divide and fill the layers. (See instructions on p. 19: 'Filling and coating cakes'.)

2. Coat the cakes with plain or chocolate buttercream icing or white or dark chocolate ganache coating.

3. Stack the cakes using wooden skewers in the bottom tier, according to the method for stacking cakes on p. 21.

4. Spread the 100 g (3½ oz) melted dark or white chocolate on the back of each stripe before pressing it onto the cake, making sure to vary the colour and size of each stripe. Start with the top tier first, the bottom tier last.

5. Decorate your cake board, following the method on p. 22: 'Decorating a cake board'.

6. Push a toothpick into the stem of each rose and push the toothpick into the cake, or decorate with fresh red berries.

Tip

Keep the melted chocolate warm on a hot tray set at its lowest setting, placed on top of a double-folded dishcloth, or periodically reheat the chocolate in the microwave oven at 50% power for 10 seconds whenever the chocolate starts to set on the side of the bowl.

Flaky shavings and lilies

Layers of shaved chocolate look almost like flaky pastry. The chocolate paste arum lilies round off this cake suitably for a wedding.

Makes up to 70 servings.

Flaky shavings ★★★

The shavings for this project are made with 500 g (1 lb) white chocolate altogether. Melt only a ¼ of the chocolate at a time or melt it all and keep the melted chocolate warm on a hot tray set at its lowest setting, on top of a double-folded dish cloth; or periodically reheat the chocolate in the microwave oven at 50% power for 10 seconds at a time. Make sure that your cake is prepared and ready to be decorated before starting as these shavings have to be put onto the cake immediately after being made.

1. Pour about 125 ml (4½ fl oz/½ cup) of the melted white chocolate onto your working surface (a marble slab, flat tile, thick rectangular glass plate, stainless steel counter or granite worktop). You can put your marble slab, flat tile or glass plate in the refrigerator for 10 minutes to speed up the cooling of the chocolate.

2. Spread the chocolate with a dough or metal scraper or palette knife until it cools slightly and becomes thicker. Then spread it flat into a thin layer.

3. While you wait for the chocolate to set, clean the excess chocolate off the scraper or palette knife with a sharp knife.

4. Press your finger on the chocolate – if it still feels slightly warm but does not leave a fingerprint, it is ready to use.

5. Hold a sharp knife or palette knife parallel to the surface of the worktop and scrape or slice the chocolate from the worktop from one side to the other in one motion so that it forms a big shaving.

6. Pick up the chocolate with both hands and fold it around the smaller cake on the top tier so that the shaving stands about 2.5 cm (1 in.) higher than the cake.

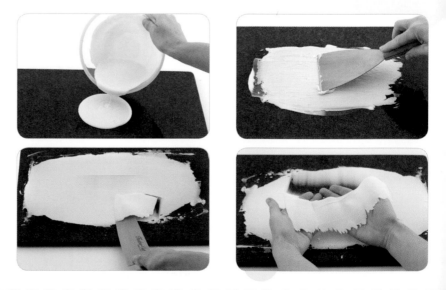

7. Keep on making shavings as before and keep on pressing them over the previous pieces onto the cake until the top cake is covered.

8. Repeat the whole process for the bottom cake until the whole cake is covered.

9. If some of the pieces feel slightly loose, pour some melted chocolate into a Ziploc bag and pipe some chocolate in between the layers and cake.

10. Scrape the leftover hardened chocolate from your counter top and remelt to make more shavings.

Chocolate paste arum lilies ★

Yellow and green were used as the colour scheme for these arum lilies. Of course you can change the colour to white lilies with yellow centres for a more traditional look.

1. Make a batch of white chocolate paste from the recipe on p. 148. Divide the paste in half and colour one half with a few drops of green colouring for a light green shade, and the other half with a few drops of yellow colouring for a light yellow shade.

2. Break off a piece of paste of about 60 g (2 oz) from each colour and divide each piece evenly into 6 balls the size of a marble or about 10 g (⅓ oz) each. These will become the centres for 12 lilies.

3. Roll each ball into a long cone shape. Dust your hands with icing (confectioner's) sugar if the paste becomes too sticky.

4. Use a toothpick to make small marks on the cones to resemble pollen.

5. Put the cones on greaseproof paper and place in the refrigerator until you are ready to use them.

6. Divide the rest of the coloured paste evenly into 6 balls for each colour, the size of a walnut or about 20 g (⅔ oz).

7. Roll each ball into a cone shape and flatten each cone on a piece of greaseproof paper or inside a plastic bag by pressing it with your fingers, a rolling pin or glass bottle.

8. Shape arum lily petals with a pointed side and flatten the edges with your fingers. Squeeze the tip of the pointed side between your fingers.

9. If the paste becomes too soft, place the petals in the refrigerator for 5 minutes to harden.

10. Dab some water on the rounded edge of a petal and fold it over the centre. Use yellow petals with green centres and green petals with yellow centres.

11. Lay all the arum lilies on a piece of sponge so that they keep their shape while they harden.

Make the complete cake ★★★

- ✓ 2 round cakes (each 2 layers) of different sizes: 25 cm (10 in.) and 15 cm (6 in.)
- ✓ 1 round 35 cm (14 in.) cake board, plywood board or cake stand
- ✓ 1 round 15 cm (6 in.) divider made from thick cardboard or foamalite, wrapped in aluminium foil or plastic cling wrap
- ✓ 2 batches of plain buttercream icing (recipe pg. 140) or 2 batches each of white chocolate ganache filling and coating (recipes p. 142 and p. 144)
- ✓ Flaky shavings made from 500 g (1 lb) white chocolate
- ✓ 100 g (3½ oz) white chocolate melted, to attach loose pieces
- ✓ Arum lilies made from 1 batch of white chocolate paste (see recipe p. 148):
    - 1 recipe white chocolate paste:
        - 300 g (10½ oz) white chocolate
        - 60 ml (4 tbsp) golden syrup or glucose syrup
        - 10 ml (2 tsp) water

Assembling and decorating the cake

1. Divide, fill and coat each cake with plain buttercream icing or white chocolate ganache coating. (See instructions on p. 19: 'Filling and coating cakes'.)

2. Stack the cakes using wooden skewers in the bottom tier, according to the method for stacking cakes on p. 21.

3. Decorate with flaky shavings according to the method described, starting with the top tier.

4. Decorate your cake board, following the method on p. 22: 'Decorating a cake board'.

5. Place arum lilies on top of the cake, on the bottom tier and the cake board.

Mini cakes ★★

1. Remove the paper wrappers from your cupcakes and stick two cupcakes together with filling.

2. Cover with buttercream icing or ganache coating.

3. Place chocolate shavings around each mini cake.

4. Decorate the top with a small chocolate paste arum lily.

Lace and collar

This elegant cake combines old lace with a modern straight collar and will be ideal for a wedding.

Makes up to 70 servings.

Lace and collar ★★★

In this project, each tier has a collar with a delicate, lacy upper edge. The collar is made in two steps.

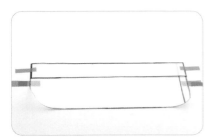

1. Make templates for each of the two collars by measuring the height and circumference of each tier.
2. Add 5 cm (2 in.) to each height measurement and 5 cm (2 in.) to each circumference measurement. Cut two pieces of greaseproof paper to these new measurements.
3. Place the smallest template on a flat surface, using adhesive tape or masking tape to make a handle for each end and to keep the paper in place.
4. Cut another strip of greaseproof paper 5 cm (2 in.) wide and the same length as the first template. This will be used to hide part of the template so that the solid collar can be cast first, and the lacy upper edge later.
5. Place the strip of paper over the first template so that it covers the top part of the paper and stick it down with adhesive tape.
6. Melt 1.2 kg (2 lb 10 oz) white chocolate. Pour 125 ml (4½ fl oz/½ cup) of the melted chocolate into a Ziploc bag and set aside to use later for making the lacy part of the collar.
7. Pour ⅓ or about 350 g (12½ oz) of the rest of the melted chocolate onto the paper in a thick line, keeping the rest warm for making the second collar.
8. Quickly spread the chocolate with a palette knife from side to side and keep on spreading from one side to the other, keeping a 2.5 cm (1 in.) strip of paper open at one end. Spread the chocolate slightly over the edges of the paper because the chocolate on the edges always sets more quickly than the chocolate in the middle. By keeping the chocolate moving, you regulate the temperature for the chocolate to set more evenly. Keep on spreading until the chocolate starts to thicken and set slightly. If you are using eating chocolate only, this can take up to 30 minutes.

9. Quickly remove the thin strip of paper hiding part of the template, also lifting any chocolate adhering to it. You are now ready to pipe the lacy upper edge with the chocolate in the Ziploc bag. Snip off a corner of the Ziploc bag.

10. Pipe the chocolate over the formed chocolate collar and onto the clean strip of the template by swirling the chocolate in circles in a lace pattern. If the solid collar starts to set too quickly, before you are ready for piping, use a hairdryer to blow hot air over the chocolate to remelt it slightly.

11. Wait for the lace to set slightly but make sure that the rest of the collar does not become too firm. If the chocolate is slightly set but still warm, with some chocolate coming off onto your finger, the collar is ready to be lifted.

12. Quickly lift the paper off the work surface by holding the clean strip at one end and the adhesive tape at the other end. Press the collar onto the cake with the chocolate side against the cake and the paper on the outside.

13. Use your hands to guide the paper all the way around the cake and fold one edge over the other.

14. Place the cake with the collar in the refrigerator for 10 minutes.

15. When the fitted collar has set, carefully remove the paper. Where the ends of the paper meet, slowly wriggle out the paper from under the top chocolate seam.

16. With a sharp knife or pizza wheel, carefully cut off the overlapping chocolate seam so that the two ends meet neatly.

17. Make the other collar in the same way, cutting a strip of greaseproof paper to hide the upper edge of the template. Using the remaining melted chocolate, first make the solid collar and then add the upper lacy collar.

Make the complete cake ★★★

- ✓ 2 round cakes (2 layers each) of different sizes: 25 cm (10 in.) and 15 cm (6 in.)
- ✓ 1 round 35 cm (14 in.) cake board, plywood board or cake stand
- ✓ 1 round 15 cm (6 in.) divider made from thick cardboard or foamalite, wrapped in aluminium foil or plastic cling wrap
- ✓ 2 batches of plain buttercream icing (recipe p. 140) or 2 batches each of white chocolate ganache filling and coating (recipes p. 142 and p. 144)
- ✓ Lace and collar made with 1.2 kg (2½ lb) white chocolate
- ✓ 30 – 40 white and dark chocolate truffles (see recipe on p. 146)
- ✓ 8 – 10 fresh flowers such as gerberas

Assembling and decorating the cake

1. Divide, fill and coat each cake with plain buttercream icing or white chocolate ganache. (See instructions on p. 19: 'Filling and coating cakes'.)
2. Stack the cakes using wooden skewers in the bottom tier, according to the method for stacking cakes on p. 21.
3. Starting with the topmost, smallest tier, make and fit one lacy collar at a time.

4. Decorate your cake board, following the method on p. 22: 'Decorating a cake board'.
5. Decorate the truffles with coloured chocolate stripes in your colour scheme, for instance red, pink and orange.
6. When the chocolate stripes have set, add the truffles to the top of each cake tier and the cake board. Be very careful when putting the truffles onto the cake as the lace collar is extremely fragile.
7. Decorate with fresh flowers in the colour scheme of your choice.

Mini cakes ★★

1. Remove the paper wrappers from your cupcakes and stick two cupcakes together with filling.
2. Place the mini cakes in the refrigerator for an hour, making them easier to cut.
3. Slice a sliver from all sides to make the mini cakes even all round.
4. Cover with buttercream icing or ganache coating.
5. Take the measurements of one mini cake and use that to make templates for all of them.
6. Make a lacy collar for each mini cake, following the instructions above.
7. Decorate with a chocolate truffle.

Wrinkled layered collar

Layers and layers of chocolate and magical twirly whirlys! What more could one wish for, especially if the cake is personalized with your own initials …

Makes up to 100 servings.

Wrinkled collars ★★★

- This impressive cake has double layers of chocolate collars. The collar for each tier is made separately in two steps and has to cool and set before the next one is made. Ensure that you have enough room in your refrigerator for the whole cake by removing some of the racks if necessary.
- If you make a smaller cake, adjust the amounts as needed.

1. To make templates for each of the four collars, measure the height and circumference of each tier.
2. Add 2.5 cm (1 in.) to each height measurement and 10 cm (4 in.) to each circumference measurement.
3. For each collar, cut two templates from greaseproof paper:
   - One template according to the new measurement (paper 1) which will form the foundation.
   - A second template with half the height and the same length as the first paper (paper 2) which will be used over the foundation.
4. Melt 1.2 kg (2½ lb) dark chocolate for the foundation collars.
5. Melt 600 g (1¼ lb) white chocolate for the uppermost collars and colour it to your liking, e.g. light blue, by mixing 10 ml (2 tsp) vegetable oil with 30 drops or 2.5 ml (½ tsp) blue liquid food colouring or a few drops (¼ tsp) paste food colouring.

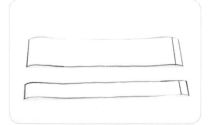

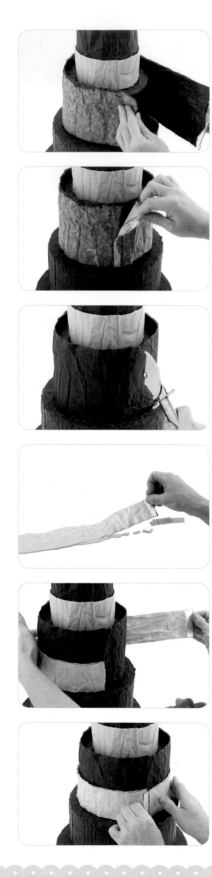

6. Starting with the templates for the smallest tier on top, take each template in both hands and crush it to form wrinkles. The added 10 cm (4 in.) to the circumference will make up for the wrinkling of the paper.

7. Fold open the larger of the two templates (paper 1) and place on a flat surface, using adhesive tape or masking tape to make a handle for each end and to keep the paper in place. Measure the length again to ensure that it is still long enough to go around the cake.

8. Pour some of the melted dark chocolate onto the paper in a thick line.

9. Quickly spread the chocolate with a palette knife from side to side and keep on spreading from one side to the other. Keeping a 2.5 cm (1 in.) strip of paper open on one side by which you will later pick up the template. Spread the chocolate over the edges of the paper because the chocolate on the edges always sets more quickly than the chocolate in the middle. By keeping the chocolate moving, you regulate the temperature for the chocolate to set more evenly. Keep on spreading until the chocolate starts to thicken and set slightly. If you are using eating chocolate only, this step may take up to 30 minutes.

10. Touch the surface of the chocolate with your finger. If the chocolate is slightly firm but still warm, with some chocolate coming off onto your finger, the collar is ready to be lifted.

11. Quickly lift the paper off the work surface by holding the clean strip at one end and the adhesive tape at the other end. Press the collar onto the cake with the chocolate side against the cake and the paper on the outside.

12. Use your hands to guide the paper all the way around the cake and fold one edge over the other.

13. Place the cake with the collar in the refrigerator for 10 minutes.

14. When the fitted collar has set, carefully remove the paper. Where the ends of the paper meet, slowly wriggle out the paper from under the top chocolate seam.

15. With a sharp knife or pizza wheel, carefully cut off the overlapping chocolate seam so that the two ends meet neatly.

16. Dab some melted chocolate on the inside of the collar where the seam meets, to seal the join.

17. Now start with the second collar for the top tier, using the smaller wrinkled template (paper 2). Fold it open on the work surface, making sure that it is still long enough to go around the cake and secure with tape.

18. Pour some of the melted blue chocolate onto the paper in a thick line and, using the same method as before, proceed to spread the chocolate until it has nearly set and you can lift and fit the collar around the first, dark chocolate collar.

19. Place the cake in the refrigerator for 5 – 10 minutes to let the chocolate cool and set completely.

20. Remove the cake from the refrigerator. Remove the paper, cut off the overlapping seam and seal the join. The first tier has been completed!

21. Now repeat all the steps for the other three tiers, fitting two collars around each and ending with the largest, bottom tier.

Chocolate twirly whirlys ★★

1. Cut a few thin strips of greaseproof paper, e.g. 2.5 cm (1 in.) x 20 cm (8 in.).

2. Melt 100 g (3½ oz) dark chocolate.

3. Spread some melted chocolate onto the strips of paper, wait until the chocolate sets slightly, and then scrape the chocolate with a wide-toothed comb so that grooves form. Then twist the strips into spirals using your hands.

4. Place all the spirals on greaseproof paper on a baking tin or wooden tray that will fit into your refrigerator.

5. When your tray is full or all the chocolate has been used, place the tray with the spirals in the refrigerator for no longer than 10 minutes for the chocolate to set and harden.

6. Remove the tray from the refrigerator and carefully pull the paper off the chocolate spirals.

7. Carefully twist the spirals loose from each other.

Chocolate initials ★

1. Make a template for the initials by drawing your chosen initials on a normal sheet of paper and place it on a baking tin or wooden tray.

2. Cut greaseproof paper to cover your template and secure it with adhesive tape.

3. Melt 50 g (2 oz) white chocolate and colour it with your choice of colour, e.g. light blue, by mixing 1.25 ml (¼ tsp) vegetable oil with 3 drops of blue liquid food colouring or a few drops of paste food colouring.

4. Pour the coloured chocolate into a Ziploc bag and snip off a corner to make a piping bag.

5. Pipe an outline of the initial onto the paper.

6. Place a wooden skewer cut in half into each initial.

7. Fill in the outline with more melted chocolate.

8. Before the chocolate sets, place dragees on the initial.

9. Place the tray in the refrigerator for 10 minutes for the chocolate to set.

10. Remove the tray from the refrigerator. Take hold of the sticks and carefully pull the chocolate initials off the paper.

Make the complete cake ★★★

- ✓ 4 round cakes (2 layers each) of different sizes: 25 cm (10 in.), 20 cm (8 in.), 15 cm (6 in.) and 10 cm (4 in.)
- ✓ 1 round 35 cm (14 in.) cake board, plywood board or cake stand
- ✓ 3 round cake boards or dividers made from thick cardboard or foamalite, wrapped in aluminium foil or plastic cling wrap, of 20 cm (8 in.), 15 cm (6 in.) and 10 cm (4 in.)
- ✓ 3½ batches of chocolate buttercream icing (recipe p. 141) or 3½ batches each of dark chocolate ganache filling and coating (recipes p. 142 and p. 144)
- ✓ Wrinkled collars made with:
     - 1.2 kg (2½ lb) dark chocolate
     - 600 g (1¼ lb) white chocolate
     - 10 ml (2 tsp) vegetable oil
     - 30 drops or 2.5 ml (½ tsp) blue liquid food colouring
- ✓ Chocolate twirly whirlys made with 100 g (3½ oz) dark chocolate
- ✓ Chocolate initials made with:
     - 50 g (2 oz) white chocolate
     - 1.25 ml (¼ tsp) vegetable oil
     - 3 drops of blue liquid food colouring
     - Dragees (candy beads)

Assembling and decorating the cake

1. Divide, fill and coat each cake with chocolate buttercream icing or dark chocolate ganache. (See instructions on p. 19: 'Filling and coating cakes'.)
2. Stack the tiers using wooden skewers, following the method described on p. 21.
3. Make and fit the collars for each tier, finishing each collar individually before making the next. Work from the top of the cake downwards.
4. Decorate the cake with twirly whirlys and push the chocolate initials into the top of the cake.

Mini cakes ★★

1. Remove the paper wrappers from your cupcakes and stick two cupcakes together with filling.
2. Slice a sliver from all sides to make the mini cakes even all round.
3. Cover with buttercream icing or ganache coating.
4. Take the measurements of one mini cake to make templates for them all.
5. Make double collars for each mini cake, following the instructions above.
6. Decorate with twirly whirlys.

Basic recipes

Before you start baking

I want to share an important tip with you on baking cakes successfully: LINE YOUR BAKING TINS! You might sigh and think this is an unnecessary time-consuming bother, but in the long run it will save you time and money:

- Batter will not spill in the oven, causing smoke and ruined, bitter-tasting cakes.
- Easy to turn cakes out of the tins without breaking.
- Tins are ready to be used again immediately.
- No need to wash tins, prolonging the lifespan of the non-stick lining and preventing rust.

1. Measure the circumference and height of your cake tins.
2. Cut a piece of greaseproof paper for each tin, 5 cm (2 in.) higher than the tin and slightly longer than the circumference to overlap when fitting into the tin.
3. Fold over 2.5 cm (1 in.) on one long edge of each strip and cut this flap at regular intervals. The cuts make the paper fit more easily.
4. Trace the tin bottoms onto greaseproof paper and cut out.
5. Place the rectangular greaseproof strips inside the tins with the cut flap eased on the bottom and place the bottom pieces on top of the flap so that they fit snugly and the tins are fully lined.
6. Spray the paper with non-stick cooking spray.
7. Follow these instructions for round, square or rectangular tins.

Serving guide

How many servings can you expect from a cake? Use the serving guide to work out how much cake you need. Calculations were based on 10 cm (4 in.) high cake tiers.

Size Metric cm:	Size Imperial in.:	Round cake serves:	Square cake serves:
10	4	8	10
15	6	12	20
20	8	24	40
22	9	36	50
25	10	48	60
30	12	60	80
35	14	84	100
Tiered cake:			
15 + 20 + 25	6 + 8 + 10	100 – 120	120 – 150
15 + 22 + 30	6 + 9 + 12	120 – 150	150 – 200
15 + 20 + 25 + 30	6 + 8 + 10 + 12	150 – 200	200 – 250

Note: Any round or square cake is usually baked in two baking tins, yielding two layers each about 5 cm (2 in.) high. Each layer can be sliced and filled with buttercream, yielding four layers, which, stuck on top of each other, form a whole cake, 10 cm (4 in.) or more high. This cake becomes a tier when stacked with other cakes in a many-tiered cake.

White chocolate mud cake

This is a moist white chocolate cake with a dense, fudgy texture and is quite sweet. It is not necessary to fill this cake as it has enough moistness but if you want it to be extra decadent, fill with buttercream, ganache, caramel, cream or jam.

This recipe makes two 20 cm (8 in.) round cake layers each 5 cm (2 in.) high. For other sizes, consult the table opposite.

Ingredients

- ✓ 300 g (10½ oz) white chocolate, broken into pieces
- ✓ 500 g (1 lb 2 oz) salted butter
- ✓ 800 g (1 lb 12½ oz) white sugar
- ✓ 500 ml (18 fl oz/2 cups) full cream milk
- ✓ 450 g (1 lb) cake flour
- ✓ 150 g (5½ oz) self-raising flour
- ✓ 4 large eggs, lightly beaten
- ✓ 10 ml (2 tsp) vanilla essence

Note: The top of the cake tends to crack. This crunchy layer can be sliced off or left as is, whichever you prefer.

Method

1. Preheat the oven to 160 °C (325 °F) for a conventional oven or 150 °C (300 °F) for a fan-assisted oven.

2. Line the base and sides of two 20 cm (8 in.) round cake tins with greaseproof paper and spray with non-stick cooking spray (see instructions on p. 124: 'Before you start baking').

3. Assemble your ingredients.

4. Mix the chocolate, butter, sugar and milk together in a bowl and heat in the microwave oven at 100% power. Stir well at 2-minute intervals until the mixture is melted and smooth. Let the mixture cool for 20 minutes.

5. Sift the flours and add the lightly beaten eggs, vanilla essence and the cooled chocolate mixture.

6. Pour equal amounts of batter into the two lined tins and bake for about an hour and 50 minutes or until an inserted skewer comes out clean.

7. Let the cakes cool in the tins, preferably overnight.

8. Turn the cakes out of the tins and tear off the greaseproof paper.

9. Divide each cake into two layers. Sewing thread or dental floss does an excellent job of slicing through the cake neatly (see instructions on p. 19: 'Filling and coating cakes').

10. Spread three of the layers with buttercream icing or ganache filling, stack layers on top of each other and cover the top and outside of the cake with buttercream icing or ganache coating. (See recipes for buttercream icing and ganache filling and coating on pp. 140 – 145.)

Adjusting the recipe

Metric: The cake recipes are all for a 20 cm round cake 10 cm high baked in two layers. However, it is easy to adjust the basic recipe by the following amounts for different-sized cake tins:

Round tins (2):	15 cm	18 cm	20 cm	22 cm	25 cm	28 cm	30 cm	35 cm
Square tins (2):	12 cm	15 cm	18 cm	20 cm	22 cm	25 cm	28 cm	30 cm
Rectangular tin (1):			23 x 30 cm					
Recipe amount:	½	¾	1	1¼	1½	2	2½	3

Imperial: The cake recipes are all for an 8 in round cake 4 in high baked in two layers. However, it is easy to adjust the basic recipe by the following amounts for different-sized cake tins:

Round tins (2):	6 in.	7 in.	8 in.	9 in.	10 in.	11 in.	12 in.	14 in.
Square tins (2):	5 in.	6 in.	7 in.	8 in.	9 in.	10 in.	11 in.	12 in.
Rectangular tin (1):			9 x 12 in.					
Recipe amount:	½	¾	1	1¼	1½	2	2½	3

Of course you have to adjust the baking time as well. Bake larger cakes for a longer time and smaller cakes for less time:

- For each 5 cm (2 in.) difference in tin size, bake ±20 minutes longer or shorter.

Variations of white chocolate mud cake

When making smaller or larger cakes, adjust these variations according to recipe amounts.

Orange white chocolate mud cake

- Add the grated zest of an orange to the batter.
- Use the juice of the orange with the milk to make up the liquid amount to 500 ml (18 fl oz/2 cups).
- Replace the vanilla essence with 10 ml (2 tsp) orange essence or orange blossom water.

Tips

- A filled white chocolate cake will keep for 4 days at room temperature or 6 days in the refrigerator.
- It can also be frozen, filled or unfilled, for up to 3 months.

Lemon white chocolate mud cake

- Add the grated zest of a lemon to the batter.
- Use the juice of the lemon with the milk to make up the liquid amount to 500 ml (18 fl oz/2 cups).
- Replace the vanilla essence with 10 ml (2 tsp) lemon essence.

Coffee white chocolate mud cake

- Mix 60 ml (4 tbsp) instant coffee granules with the milk before adding it to the chocolate, butter and sugar to be melted.
- Use light or dark brown sugar instead of white sugar.

Caramel white chocolate mud cake

- Use dark brown sugar instead of white sugar.
- Replace the vanilla essence with caramel essence.

Liqueur white chocolate mud cake

- Mix 60 ml (4 tbsp) of your favourite liqueur or brandy with the milk to make up the liquid amount to 500 ml (18 fl oz/2 cups).

Double chocolate white mud cake

- Add 100 g (3½ oz) dark or caramel chocolate chips to the batter (coat the chocolate chips with some flour so that they do not sink to the bottom of the tin).

Crunchy nutty white chocolate mud cake

- Chop 100 g (3½ oz) of your favourite nuts and add to the batter (coat the nuts with some flour so that they do not sink to the bottom of the tin).

Coconut white chocolate mud cake

- Use coconut milk instead of the full cream milk and coconut essence instead of the vanilla essence.
- Add 250 ml (9 fl oz/1 cup) shredded coconut to the batter.

Turkish delight white chocolate mud cake

- Replace the vanilla essence with rose water and add 100 g (3½ oz) chopped Turkish delight sweets to the batter (coat the Turkish delight with some flour so that the pieces do not sink to the bottom of the tin.

Dark chocolate mud cake

This is a rich dark chocolate cake. If you ever master only one chocolate cake recipe, this one would be worth the effort as it's the only recipe you will ever need! You do not have to fill this cake as it is sweet and sticky on the inside, but if you want to give the cake an extra dimension, then fill with buttercream or chocolate ganache.

This recipe makes two 20 cm (8 in.) round cake layers each 5 cm (2 in.) high. For other sizes, consult the table in 'Adjusting the recipe'.

Ingredients

- ✓ 380 g (13½ oz) dark chocolate, broken into pieces
- ✓ 380 g (13½ oz) salted butter
- ✓ 40 ml (8 tsp) instant coffee granules
- ✓ 280 ml (10 fl oz) water
- ✓ 220 g (8 oz) cake flour
- ✓ 220 g (8 oz) self-raising flour
- ✓ 80 g (3 oz) cocoa powder
- ✓ 2.5 ml (½ tsp) bicarbonate of soda
- ✓ 840 g (1 lb 14 oz) white sugar
- ✓ 6 large eggs
- ✓ 60 ml (4 tbsp) vegetable oil
- ✓ 190 ml (7 fl oz) buttermilk
- ✓ 10 ml (2 tsp) vanilla essence

Method

1. Preheat the oven to 160 °C (325 °F) for a conventional oven or 150 °C (300 °F) for a fan-assisted oven.

2. Line the base and sides of two 20 cm (8 in.) round cake tins with grease-proof paper and spray with non-stick cooking spray (see instructions on p. 124: 'Before you start baking').

3. Assemble your ingredients.

4. Mix chocolate pieces, butter, coffee granules and water together in a bowl and heat in the microwave oven at 50% power for 2-minute intervals. Stir well at every interval until the mixture is melted and smooth. Let the mixture cool for 20 minutes.

5. Sift the flours, cocoa powder and bicarbonate of soda together into a large bowl and stir the sugar into the flour mix.

6. Mix eggs, vegetable oil, buttermilk and vanilla essence together in another bowl.

7. Stir the egg mixture and the cooled chocolate mixture into the flour and mix until smooth and lump-free.

8. Pour equal amounts of batter into the two lined tins and bake for about an hour and 40 minutes or until an inserted skewer comes out clean.

9. Let the cakes cool in the tins, preferably overnight.

10. Turn the cakes out of the tins and tear off the greaseproof paper.

11. Divide each cake into two layers. Sewing thread or dental floss does an excellent job of slicing through the cake neatly (see instructions on p. 19: 'Filling and coating cakes').

12. Spread three of the layers with buttercream icing or ganache filling, stack layers on top of each other and cover the top and outside of the cake with buttercream icing or ganache coating. (See recipes for buttercream icing and ganache filling and coating on pp. 140 – 145.)

Adjusting the recipe

Metric: The cake recipes are all for a 20 cm round cake 10 cm high baked in two layers. However, it is easy to adjust the basic recipe by the following amounts for different-sized cake tins:

Round tins (2):	15 cm	18 cm	20 cm	22 cm	25 cm	28 cm	30 cm	35 cm
Square tins (2):	12 cm	15 cm	18 cm	20 cm	22 cm	25 cm	28 cm	30 cm
Rectangular tin (1):			23 x 30 cm					
Recipe amount:	½	¾	1	1¼	1½	2	2½	3

Imperial: The cake recipes are all for an 8 in round cake 4 in high baked in two layers. However, it is easy to adjust the basic recipe by the following amounts for different-sized cake tins:

Round tins (2):	6 in.	7 in.	8 in.	9 in.	10 in.	11 in.	12 in.	14 in.
Square tins (2):	5 in.	6 in.	7 in.	8 in.	9 in.	10 in.	11 in.	12 in.
Rectangular tin (1):			9 x 12 in.					
Recipe amount:	½	¾	1	1¼	1½	2	2½	3

Of course you have to adjust the baking time as well. Bake larger cakes for a longer time and smaller cakes for less time:

• For each 5 cm (2 in.) difference in tin size, bake ±20 minutes longer or shorter.

Variations of dark chocolate mud cake

When making smaller or larger cakes, adjust these variations according to recipe amounts.

Orange dark chocolate mud cake

- Add the grated zest of an orange to the batter.
- Use the juice of the orange with the buttermilk to make up the liquid amount to 190 ml (7 fl oz).
- Replace the vanilla essence with 10 ml (2 tsp) orange essence or orange blossom water.

Liqueur dark chocolate mud cake

- Mix 60 ml (4 tbsp) of your favourite liqueur or brandy with the buttermilk to make up the liquid amount to 190 ml (7 fl oz).

Double chocolate mud cake

- Add 100 g (3½ oz) white or caramel chocolate chips to the batter (coat the chocolate chips with some flour so that they do not sink to the bottom).

Crunchy nutty dark chocolate mud cake

- Chop 100 g (3½ oz) of your favourite nuts and add to the batter (coat the nuts with some flour so that they do not sink to the bottom).

Tips

- A filled dark chocolate mud cake will keep for 5 days at room temperature or 7 days in the refrigerator.
- It can also be frozen, filled or unfilled, for up to 3 months.

Chocolate chip cupcakes

Cupcakes are extremely versatile as you can use them for children's birthday parties and even for elegant weddings, depending on their decoration. This recipe is quick and easy and the cupcakes are light and buttery.

This recipe makes 12 cupcakes. Double or triple the recipe for more cupcakes.

Ingredients

- ✓ 125 g (4½ oz) self-raising flour
- ✓ 1 tsp (5 ml) baking powder
- ✓ 125 g (4½ oz) white sugar
- ✓ 125 g (4½ oz) salted butter, softened
- ✓ 2 large eggs
- ✓ 2 tbsp (30 ml) milk
- ✓ 1 tsp (5 ml) vanilla essence
- ✓ 50 g (2 oz) white, caramel or dark chocolate chips
- ✓ 12 normal sized muffin paper cups

Method

1. Preheat a conventional oven to 170 °C (350 °F).
2. Assemble your ingredients.
3. Sift the flour and baking powder together in a mixing bowl. Add the sugar, butter and eggs. Use an electric mixer and mix for 30 seconds.
4. Add the milk and vanilla essence and beat for another 30 seconds.
5. Fold the chocolate chips into the cupcake batter.
6. Place 12 muffin paper cups into a muffin tray and spoon equal amounts of batter into the cups using an ice-cream scoop.
7. Bake for 20 minutes or until the cupcakes are golden on top and an inserted skewer or toothpick comes out clean.
8. Cool the cupcakes on a wire cooling rack.

9. When cool, remove from the rack and spread generously with buttercream icing or ganache coating; or melt some ganache coating in the microwave oven until runny and dip the cupcakes into it. (See recipes for buttercream icing and ganache coating on pp. 140 – 145.)

10. Place decorations on top of the cupcakes.

Variation

Double chocolate chip cupcakes

- Mix 30 ml (2 tbsp) cocoa powder with 30 ml (2 tbsp) boiling water and let it cool slightly. Add this to the flour mixture at the beginning of the recipe.

Tips

- Un-iced cupcakes can be kept for two days in an airtight container at room temperature or frozen for up to two months.
- Iced cupcakes will last for 4 days at room temperature.

Cupcake wrappers

An inventive way to dress up your cupcakes is to use individual wrappers.

1. Copy the cupcake wrapper template on p. 158 onto paper to use as a cutting guide.
2. Use the cut-out template to trace the cupcake wrappers with pencil onto any thick paper or thin cardboard and cut out. You should be able to cut three wrappers from an A4-sized sheet or four wrappers from a scrapbooking sheet.
3. You can add a scalloped edge or cut it with scrapbooking scissors.
4. Fold the wrapper, put double-sided adhesive tape or non-toxic glue onto one edge and paste the ends together.
5. Place iced cupcakes into the wrappers.

Chocolate fruitcake

This modern chocolate version of a traditional fruitcake is rich and moist and will last longer than any other chocolate cake.

This recipe makes two 20 cm (8 in.) round cake layers each 5 cm (2 in.) high. For other sizes, consult the table opposite.

Ingredients

- ✓ 1.1 kg (2 lb 7 oz) mixed dried fruit of your choice
- ✓ 240 g (8½ oz) salted butter
- ✓ 15 ml (1 tbsp) instant coffee granules
- ✓ 400 ml (14 fl oz) water
- ✓ 240 g (8½ oz) brown sugar
- ✓ 250 ml (9 fl oz/1 cup) golden syrup
- ✓ 250 ml (9 fl oz/1 cup) brandy (or more water)
- ✓ 100 g (3½ oz) slivered almonds (optional)
- ✓ 60 g (2 oz) cocoa
- ✓ 300 g (10½ oz) cake flour, sifted
- ✓ 2.5 ml (½ tsp) baking powder
- ✓ 2.5 ml (½ tsp) bicarbonate of soda
- ✓ 4 large eggs, beaten

Method

1. Preheat the oven to 150 °C (300 °F) for a conventional oven or 140 °C (275 °F) for a fan-assisted oven.

2. Line the base and sides of two 20 cm (8 in.) round cake tins with grease-proof paper and spray with non-stick cooking spray (see instructions on p. 124: 'Before you start baking').

3. Put three layers of newspaper around the outside of the tins up to where the greaseproof paper ends and tie with string or kitchen twine.

4. Assemble your ingredients.

5. Put the mixed fruit, butter, coffee granules, water, brown sugar, golden syrup, brandy and optional slivered almonds into a pot and bring to the boil on the stove on medium heat, stirring frequently. Boil for 5 minutes.

6. Remove from the heat and let it cool for 40 minutes or until it reaches room temperature.

7. Sift together the cocoa powder, cake flour, baking powder and bicarbonate of soda.

8. Add the flour mixture and the beaten eggs to the cooled fruit mixture and mix well.

9. Pour equal amounts of batter into the two lined tins and bake for about an hour and 30 minutes or until an inserted skewer comes out clean.

10. Let the cakes cool in the tins, preferably overnight.

11. Turn the cakes out of the tins and tear off the greaseproof paper.

12. Do not divide the cakes into layers but keep them whole.

13. Spread one cake with chocolate buttercream icing or ganache filling, stack the other cake on top and cover the outside of the cake with chocolate buttercream icing or ganache coating. (See recipes for buttercream icing and ganache filling and coating on pp. 140 – 145.)

Adjusting the recipe

Metric: The cake recipes are all for a 20 cm round cake 10 cm high baked in two layers. However, it is easy to adjust the basic recipe by the following amounts for different-sized cake tins:

Round tins (2):	15 cm	18 cm	20 cm	22 cm	25 cm	28 cm	30 cm	35 cm
Square tins (2):	12 cm	15 cm	18 cm	20 cm	22 cm	25 cm	28 cm	30 cm
Rectangular tin (1):			23 x 30 cm					
Recipe amount:	½	¾	1	1¼	1½	2	2½	3

Imperial: The cake recipes are all for an 8 in round cake 4 in high baked in two layers. However, it is easy to adjust the basic recipe by the following amounts for different-sized cake tins:

Round tins (2):	6 in.	7 in.	8 in.	9 in.	10 in.	11 in.	12 in.	14 in.
Square tins (2):	5 in.	6 in.	7 in.	8 in.	9 in.	10 in.	11 in.	12 in.
Rectangular tin (1):			9 x 12 in.					
Recipe amount:	½	¾	1	1¼	1½	2	2½	3

Of course you have to adjust the baking time as well. Bake larger cakes for a longer time and smaller cakes for less time:

- For each 5 cm (2 in.) difference in tin size, bake ±20 minutes longer or shorter.

Variations of chocolate fruit cake

When making smaller or larger cakes, adjust these variations according to recipe amounts.

Tropical fruit cake

- Use 900 g (2 lb) mixed, light-coloured or 'tropical' fruit, e.g. sultanas, candied pineapple, candied papaya, candied coconut, dried apricots, dried pears and red glacé cherries and 200 g (7 oz) of desiccated coconut or freshly grated coconut instead of mixed dried fruit.
- Add 250 ml (9 fl oz/1 cup) Malibu rum instead of the brandy if preferred (Malibu has a slight coconut flavour, enhancing the tropical taste of your fruit cake).
- Replace the coffee granules with 10 ml (2 tsp) almond essence.

Orange chocolate fruit cake

- Add the grated zest of an orange to the fruit mixture.
- Use the juice of the orange with the water to make up the liquid amount to 375 ml (13 fl oz/1½ cups).
- Replace the coffee granules with 5 ml (1 tsp) orange essence or orange blossom water.

Lemon chocolate fruit cake

- Add the grated zest of a lemon to the fruit mixture.
- Use the juice of the lemon with the water to make up the liquid amount to 375 ml (13 fl oz/1½ cups).
- Omit the coffee granules.

Liqueur chocolate fruit cake

- Use any liqueur of your choice instead of the brandy.

Double chocolate fruit cake

- Add 100 g (3½ oz) dark, white or caramel chocolate chips to the finished mixture before pouring into the tins.

Chocolate fruit cake cupcakes

- Pour cake batter into ±36 muffin cases and bake in a conventional oven at 170 °C (350 °F) for 30 – 40 minutes or until a skewer inserted comes out clean.

Chocolate carrot cake

The best of both: carrot cake and chocolate cake combined into one, with a little less guilt.

This recipe makes two 20 cm (8 in.) round cake layers each 5 cm (2 in.) high. For other sizes, consult the table on the next page.

Ingredients

- ✓ 450 g (1 lb) brown sugar
- ✓ 6 large eggs
- ✓ 450 ml (16 fl oz/1¾ cups) vegetable oil
- ✓ 10 ml (2 tsp) vanilla essence
- ✓ 375 g (13 oz) cake flour
- ✓ 75 g (2½ oz) cocoa powder
- ✓ 7.5 ml (1½ tsp) baking powder
- ✓ 7.5 ml (1½ tsp) bicarbonate of soda
- ✓ 5 ml (1 tsp) ground cinnamon
- ✓ 450 g (1 lb) grated carrots
- ✓ 100 g (3½ oz) chopped pecan nuts

Method

1. Preheat the oven to 170 °C (350 °F) for a conventional oven or 150 °C (300 °F) for a fan-assisted oven.
2. Line the base and sides of two 20 cm (8 in.) round cake tins with grease-proof paper and spray with non-stick cooking spray (see instructions on p. 124: 'Before you start baking').
3. Assemble your ingredients.
4. Put the brown sugar, eggs and oil and vanilla essence into a mixing bowl and whisk with an electric beater until all the ingredients are combined.
5. Sift the cake flour, cocoa powder, baking powder, bicarbonate of soda and cinnamon together.
6. Add the flour mixture to the egg mixture and stir until well mixed.
7. Stir in the grated carrots and pecan nuts until evenly incorporated.
8. Pour equal amounts of batter into the two lined tins and bake for about 50 – 60 minutes or until an inserted skewer comes out clean.

9. Let the cakes cool in the tins, preferably overnight.

10. Turn the cakes out of the tins and tear off the greaseproof paper.

11. Divide each cake into two layers. Sewing thread or dental floss does an excellent job of slicing through the cake neatly (see instructions on p. 19: 'Filling and coating cakes').

12. Spread each layer with buttercream icing or ganache filling, stack layers on top of each other and cover the outside of the cake with buttercream icing or ganache coating. (See recipes for buttercream icing and ganache filling and coating on pp. 140 – 145.)

Adjusting the recipe

Metric: The cake recipes are all for a 20 cm round cake 10 cm high baked in two layers. However, it is easy to adjust the basic recipe by the following amounts for different-sized cake tins:

Round tins (2):	15 cm	18 cm	20 cm	22 cm	25 cm	28 cm	30 cm	35 cm
Square tins (2):	12 cm	15 cm	18 cm	20 cm	22 cm	25 cm	28 cm	30 cm
Rectangular tin (1):			23 x 30 cm					
Recipe amount:	½	¾	1	1¼	1½	2	2 ½	3

Imperial: The cake recipes are all for an 8 in round cake 4 in high baked in two layers. However, it is easy to adjust the basic recipe by the following amounts for different-sized cake tins:

Round tins (2):	6 in.	7 in.	8 in.	9 in.	10 in.	11 in.	12 in.	14 in.
Square tins (2):	5 in.	6 in.	7 in.	8 in.	9 in.	10 in.	11 in.	12 in.
Rectangular tin (1):			9 x 12 in.					
Recipe amount:	½	¾	1	1¼	1½	2	2 ½	3

Of course you have to adjust the baking time as well. Bake larger cakes for a longer time and smaller cakes for less time:

• For each 5 cm (2 in.) difference in tin size, bake ±20 minutes longer or shorter.

Tips

- A filled chocolate carrot cake will keep for 4 days at room temperature or 6 days in the refrigerator.
- It can also be frozen, filled or unfilled, for up to 3 months.

Variations of chocolate carrot cake

When making smaller or larger cakes, adjust these variations according to recipe amounts.

Orange chocolate carrot cake

- Add the grated zest of an orange to the cake batter.

Lemon chocolate carrot cake

- Add the grated zest of a lemon to the cake batter.

Banana chocolate carrot cake

- Add 100 g (3½ oz) mashed banana to the batter with the carrots and nuts.

Coconut chocolate carrot cake

- Add 100 g (3½ oz) grated coconut to the batter with the carrots and nuts.

Pineapple chocolate carrot cake

- Add 100 g (3½ oz) canned chopped pineapple to the batter with the carrots and nuts.

Chocolate carrot cake cupcakes

- Pour cake batter into ±36 muffin cases and bake in a conventional oven at 170 °C (350 °F) for 20 – 25 minutes or until a skewer inserted comes out clean.

Buttercream icing

This versatile rich, sweet and buttery icing can be used as a filling or covering for any type of cake.

This recipe makes a batch of icing to fill and cover a 20 cm (8 in.) cake. Adjust the amount of buttercream icing by consulting the table in 'Adjusting the recipe'.

Ingredients

- ✓ 450 g (1 lb) salted butter at room temperature
- ✓ 1.35 kg (3 lb) icing sugar, sifted
- ✓ 15 ml (1 tbsp) vanilla essence
- ✓ Up to 45 ml (3 tbsp) cooled, boiled water

Method

1. Assemble your ingredients.
2. Beat the softened butter and the sifted icing sugar together with a standing mixer or handheld mixer until light and creamy.
3. Add the vanilla essence and beat to incorporate.
4. If the consistency feels too stiff, add a few drops of boiled water until the icing is soft and spreadable.

Adjusting the recipe

Metric: The icing recipes are all for a 20 cm round cake 10 cm high baked in two layers. However, it is easy to adjust the basic recipe by the following amounts for different-sized cakes:

Round cake:	15 cm	18 cm	20 cm	22 cm	25 cm	28 cm	30 cm	35 cm
Square cake:	12 cm	15 cm	18 cm	20 cm	22 cm	25 cm	28 cm	30 cm
Rectangular cake:			23 x 30 cm					
Recipe amount:	½	¾	1	1¼	1½	2	2 ½	3

Imperial: The icing recipes are all for an 8 in round cake 4 in high baked in two layers. However, it is easy to adjust the basic recipe by the following amounts for different-sized cakes:

Round cake:	6 in.	7 in.	8 in.	9 in.	10 in.	11 in.	12 in.	14 in.
Square cake:	5 in.	6 in.	7 in.	8 in.	9 in.	10 in.	11 in.	12 in.
Rectangular cake:			9 x 12 in.					
Recipe amount:	½	¾	1	1¼	1½	2	2½	3

Variations of buttercream icing

Orange buttercream

• Add 10 ml (2 tsp) grated orange zest.

Lemon buttercream

• Add 10 ml (2 tsp) grated lemon zest.

Coffee buttercream

• Dissolve 10 ml (2 tsp) instant coffee granules in 10 ml (2 tsp) boiling water, let it cool and then add.

Chocolate buttercream

• Dissolve 125 ml (4½ fl oz/½ cup) cocoa powder in 125 ml (4½ fl oz/½ cup) boiling water, let it cool and then add.

White chocolate buttercream

• Mix 1 full recipe buttercream with 1 full recipe white chocolate ganache coating at room temperature.

Dark chocolate buttercream

• Mix 1 full recipe buttercream with 1 full recipe dark chocolate ganache coating at room temperature.

Chocolate ganache filling

Ganache filling is soft and mousse-like with a rich, chocolate flavour. Used between the layers of a cake, it is a more stable filling than chocolate mousse. The quality of the flavour relies on the quality of the chocolate used.

This recipe makes enough ganache to fill a 20 cm (8 in.) cake. Adjust the amount of ganache filling by consulting the table in 'Adjusting the recipe'.

Ingredients

✓ *375 g (13½ oz) dark, milk or white chocolate, chopped*
✓ *250 ml (9 fl oz/1 cup) cream*

Method

1. Assemble your ingredients.
2. Heat the chopped chocolate and cream together in a bowl in a microwave oven at 20% power or at the defrost setting. Stir at 2-minute intervals until the mixture is melted and smooth.
3. Refrigerate mixture until very cold or preferably overnight.
4. Beat mixture with a hand-held beater until light and fluffy (about 3 minutes).
5. Spread directly onto cake layers to sandwich the layers together.

Adjusting the recipe

Metric: The recipes for ganache filling are all for a 20 cm round cake 10 cm high baked in two layers. However, it is easy to adjust the basic recipe by the following amounts for different-sized cakes:

Round cake:	15 cm	18 cm	20 cm	22 cm	25 cm	28 cm	30 cm	35 cm
Square cake:	12 cm	15 cm	18 cm	20 cm	22 cm	25 cm	28 cm	30 cm
Rectangular cake:			23 x 30 cm					
Recipe amount:	½	¾	1	1¼	1½	2	2 ½	3

Imperial: The recipes for ganache filling are all for an 8 in round cake 4 in high baked in two layers. However, it is easy to adjust the basic recipe by the following amounts for different-sized cakes:

Round cake:	6 in.	7 in.	8 in.	9 in.	10 in.	11 in.	12 in.	14 in.
Square cake:	5 in.	6 in.	7 in.	8 in.	9 in.	10 in.	11 in.	12 in.
Rectangular cake:			9 x 12 in.					
Recipe amount:	½	¾	1	1¼	1½	2	2 ½	3

Variations of ganache filling

Orange ganache filling

- Add 10 ml (2 tsp) grated orange zest to the melted chocolate and cream mixture.

Lemon ganache filling

- Add 10 ml (2 tsp) grated lemon zest to the melted chocolate and cream mixture.

Coffee ganache filling

- Add 10 ml (2 tsp) instant coffee granules mixed with 10 ml (2 tsp) water to the chocolate and cream before melting.

Nutty ganache filling

- Add 50 g (2 oz) toasted and chopped pecan nuts or almonds to the melted chocolate and cream mixture.

Liqueur ganache filling

- Add 30 ml (2 tbsp) of your favourite liqueur to the melted chocolate and cream mixture.

Tips

- Use your leftover chocolate from decorating projects for the ganache filling.
- The filling can be refrigerated in an airtight container for up to 3 months or frozen for 6 months. Bring back to room temperature before use.

Chocolate ganache coating

Ganache coating sets fairly hard but is still easy to cut through. It makes an excellent outer coating for a cake, sealing in all the flavour and keeping the cake fresh for longer.

This recipe makes enough ganache to coat a 20 cm (8 in.) cake. Adjust the amount of ganache filling by consulting the table in 'Adjusting the recipe'.

Ingredients

- ✓ 450 g (1 lb) dark, milk or white chocolate, chopped
- ✓ 150 ml (5½ fl oz) cream

Method

1. Assemble your ingredients.
2. Heat the chopped chocolate and cream together in a bowl in a microwave oven at 20% power or at the defrost setting. Stir at 2-minute intervals until the mixture is melted and smooth.
3. Let the mixture cool down to thicken or leave overnight. If the mixture is too solid, slowly heat again in the microwave oven at 20% power or at the defrost setting for 1-minute intervals and stir until it has softened to a spreadable consistency.
4. Spread directly onto the outside of the cake to cover entirely.

Tips

- Use your leftover chocolate from decorating projects for the ganache coating.
- The coating can be refrigerated in an airtight container for up to 3 months or frozen for 6 months. Bring back to room temperature before use.

Adjusting the recipe

Metric: The recipes for ganache coating are all for a 20 cm round cake 10 cm high baked in two layers. However, it is easy to adjust the basic recipe by the following amounts for different-sized cakes:

Round cake:	15 cm	18 cm	20 cm	22 cm	25 cm	28 cm	30 cm	35 cm
Square cake:	12 cm	15 cm	18 cm	20 cm	22 cm	25 cm	28 cm	30 cm
Rectangular cake:			23 x 30 cm					
Recipe amount:	½	¾	1	1¼	1½	2	2 ½	3

Imperial: The recipes for ganache coating are all for an 8 in round cake 4 in high baked in two layers. However, it is easy to adjust the basic recipe by the following amounts for different-sized cakes:

Round cake:	6 in.	7 in.	8 in.	9 in.	10 in.	11 in.	12 in.	14 in.
Square cake:	5 in.	6 in.	7 in.	8 in.	9 in.	10 in.	11 in.	12 in.
Rectangular cake:			9 x 12 in.					
Recipe amount:	½	¾	1	1¼	1½	2	2 ½	3

Truffles

Sinful, delightful, a chocoholic's dreams come true!

This recipe makes about 40 truffles.

Filling ingredients

✓ *125 ml (4½ fl oz/½ cup) cream*
✓ *500 g (1 lb 2 oz) dark, milk or white chocolate, chopped*
✓ *15 ml (1 tbsp) golden syrup or glucose syrup (buy at your pharmacy)*
✓ *30 ml (2 tbsp) flavouring, e.g. vanilla essence, liqueur or strong coffee (optional)*

Truffle coating

✓ *500 g (1 lb 2 oz) dark, milk or white chocolate, melted*

Decoration

✓ *Shredded coconut, coloured sugar, nonpareils, coloured choco-late shavings; or*
✓ *Coloured stripes made with 100 g (3½ oz) white chocolate, melted and coloured with 2.5 ml (½ tsp) vegetable oil mixed with 5 – 10 drops of liquid food colouring or a few drops of paste food colouring (see p. 17 for instructions)*

Method

1. Assemble your ingredients.
2. Put the cream, chopped chocolate and syrup for the filling into a mixing bowl and heat in a microwave oven at 50% power. Stir at 2-minute intervals until the chocolate is melted and the mixture is smooth.
3. Stir in the chosen flavouring.
4. Refrigerate the mixture overnight.

Tips

• Use your leftover chocolate from decorating projects for the soft truffle filling. For the outer coating, use newly melted chocolate for a firm crust.
• The filling can be refrigerated in an airtight container for up to 3 months or frozen for 6 months. Bring back to room temperature before use.

5. Take the mixture out of the refrigerator and let it stand until it returns to room temperature.

6. Use a melon-baller or teaspoon to scoop out balls from the mixture and roll into round balls.

7. If some of the mixture sticks to your hands, dip your hands in icing sugar before rolling the balls.

8. Refrigerate the rolled truffles on a greaseproof paper, foil-lined baking tin or wooden tray until needed, while melting the chocolate for coating.

9. Use the same tray or line another baking tray with greaseproof paper or foil.

10. Place a teaspoonful of the melted coating chocolate into your left hand or dip your fingers into the chocolate. Take a truffle with your right hand and roll it into the chocolate on your hand until fully coated.

11. Place the coated truffle onto the lined tray.

12. Repeat until all the truffles are coated. Wait until the chocolate has set and dried. The first coating usually cracks; this is unavoidable.

13. When the chocolate on all the truffles has set, repeat the process, thereby double-dipping all the truffles. This coats the cracks and gives the truffles a smooth layer.

14. Leave the truffles to set for a few minutes.

15. If you want to decorate the truffles with nuts, coconut, coloured sugar or nonpareils, place a pinch of any of such item on the double-dipped truffles before the chocolate sets.

16. The truffles could also be rolled in coloured chocolate shavings.

17. If you want to decorate the truffles with coloured chocolate, melt and colour the 100 g (3½ oz) white chocolate and pour into a Ziploc bag. Pipe over each truffle, or use a teaspoon or fork to spread coloured stripes or circles onto the truffles.

Tips

- Keep the melted coating chocolate warm on a hot tray set at its lowest setting, on top of a double-folded dish cloth or periodically reheat the chocolate in the micro-wave oven at 50% power for 10 seconds at a time.

- The rolled, uncoated truffles can be frozen for up to 3 months. Let them thaw completely before coating with melted chocolate.

- The finished coated truffles can be stored in an airtight container for up to 3 weeks in a cool cupboard. Do not refrigerate the truffles.

Chocolate paste

Chewy chocolate fudge that is easy to mould and sculpt into decorations for your cakes.

This recipe makes ±400 g (14 oz) of paste.

Ingredients

- ✓ *300 g (10½ oz) dark, milk or white chocolate, melted according to the instructions on p. 15*
- ✓ *If using dark chocolate: 75 ml (5 tbsp) golden syrup or glucose syrup (buy at your pharmacy)*
- ✓ *If using white or milk chocolate: 60 ml (4 tbsp) golden syrup or glucose syrup (buy at your pharmacy)*
- ✓ *Liquid: 10 ml (2 tsp) water or 10 ml (2 tsp) liquid food colouring or 10 ml (2 tsp) mixture of water and food colouring*

Method

1. Assemble your ingredients.
2. Heat the golden syrup or glucose syrup with the 10 ml (2 tsp) water or food colouring, or mixture of water and food colouring, in the microwave oven at 50% power for 10 seconds only.
3. Add this mixture to the fully melted chocolate. Stir until all the ingredients are just combined.

Tips

- Use chocolate left over from decorating projects for making chocolate paste.
- Use liquid food colouring only when using white chocolate for your paste.
- If using golden syrup with white chocolate, the paste will have a golden hue which may alter the colour you add to it. Use glucose syrup if you want a whiter paste.
- If you mix food colouring into the paste after it has firmed, use latex gloves to protect your hands from getting stained.
- Latex gloves also make it easier to knead the paste as it does not stick to the gloves.

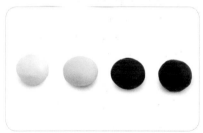

4. If liquid cocoa butter emerges from the chocolate, wipe it off with paper towels or pour the paste into a sieve and let the cocoa butter drip off. This will only happen if your ingredients are too hot.

5. Pour the paste into a plastic Ziploc bag, flatten the paste inside the bag and let it rest for a few hours or overnight at room temperature.

6. When ready to use, the paste will feel hard, so either pinch off small pieces and warm them in your hands or gently heat the ball of paste in the micro-wave oven at 20% power or on the defrost setting at 10-second intervals. Take care not to overheat the paste. If it feels too soft, place in the refrigerator for 10 minutes to firm up.

7. Knead the paste until it is pliable. Use icing sugar to dust your hands and work surface if the paste feels sticky.

8. If you did not colour the paste at the beginning or if the colour is too light, you can add colouring at this stage. If the paste softens again after mixing in the food colouring, place it in the refrigerator for 10 minutes to firm up.

9. The paste is now ready to mould into decorations.

10. If you are not using the paste immediately or if you have paste left over, wrap it in plastic cling wrap and store in a cool, dark cupboard for up to 3 weeks, or freeze for up to 6 months. Bring back to room temperature before using.

Practical advice

How to disassemble the cakes

Diagonally striped ganache with dot flowers

1. The cake can be taken apart, layer by layer, as it was assembled – use an egg-lifter to separate and remove the top layers from the bottom one.
2. Now remove the wooden skewers from the bottom layer.
3. Remove the dot flowers from each layer and set them aside to be served with the sliced cake.
4. Dip a sturdy knife into boiling water and wipe off the water with a dry cloth.
5. Cut the separate cakes into equal portions.
6. Dip the knife into the water regularly since the heated blade will ensure a neat cut.
7. Serve with a dot flower on top of each slice.

Leaves and twigs

1. The cake can be taken apart, layer by layer, as it was assembled – use an egg-lifter to separate and remove the top layers from the bottom one.
2. Now remove the wooden skewers from the bottom layer.
3. Remove the leaves from the layers and set them aside to be served with the sliced cake.
4. Dip a sturdy knife into boiling water and wipe off the water with a dry cloth.
5. Cut the separate cakes into equal portions.
6. Dip the knife into the water regularly since the heated blade will ensure a neat cut.
7. Serve with leaves on top of each slice.

Gift box

1. Carefully remove the strawberries and hearts from the box and put them aside to be served with the cake squares.
2. Dip a sturdy knife into boiling water and wipe off the water with a dry cloth.
3. Now slice the cake into equal squares by cutting between the chocolate-covered biscuits.
4. Dip the knife into the water regularly since the heated blade will ensure a neat cut.
5. Serve with strawberries and hearts on top of the squares.

Truffle tower

Allow your guests to help themselves by taking truffles from the tower.

Small shavings and bows

1. Remove the bow from the cake and set it aside.
2. Dip a sturdy knife into boiling water and wipe it with a dry cloth.
3. Starting at the top, cut each layer into 4 equal squares.
4. Alternatively, separate the layers and serve.

Chocolate rose petal cake

1. Carefully remove the large rose and the rose petals from the top of the cake.
2. Then remove the wooden skewer from the cake.
3. Remove all the chocolate petals from the sides or remove only the ones on the top layer of the cake.
4. Dip a sturdy knife into boiling water and wipe off the water with a dry cloth.
5. Cut the entire cake horizontally so that you have 2 separate layers.
6. Divide and cut each layer into 8 equal portions. If you have left some of the petals on the cake, cut through them carefully.
7. Dip the knife into the water regularly since the heated blade will ensure a neat cut.
8. Serve with rose petals and leaves on top of each slice.
9. Place the largest rose on your serving plate as a table decoration or remove the leaves one by one and serve them too.

Square cake with spirals

1. Remove the spirals on the toothpicks from the top of the cake.
2. Remove the wooden skewer.
3. Since the spirals are soft and easy to cut, you do not need to remove them.
4. Dip a sturdy knife into boiling water and wipe off the water with a dry cloth.
5. Cut the entire cake horizontally so that you have 2 separate layers.
6. Divide and cut each layer into 15 equally large squares.
7. Dip the knife into the water regularly since the heated blade will ensure a neat cut.
8. Serve the squares with extra spirals or use those on the toothpicks.

Spiky cake

1. Remove all the chocolate triangles from the cake. Alternatively, cut the cake in layers and remove the triangles from each layer.
2. Dip a sturdy knife into boiling water and wipe off the water with a dry cloth.
3. Cut the entire cake horizontally into 3 pieces, starting more or less where the separate cakes met when you had stacked the layers. You can also cut the cake piece by piece as required per serving.
4. Dip the knife into the water regularly since the heated blade will ensure a neat cut.
5. Proceed to cut the separate pieces into equal portions.
6. Serve with chocolate triangles on top of the slices.

Pleated cake with filigree decorations

1. Remove the filigree from the layers and set aside to be served with the cake squares.
2. The cake can be taken apart, layer by layer, as it was assembled – use an egg-lifter to separate and remove the top layers from the bottom one.
3. Remove the wooden skewers from the bottom layer.
4. You do not have to remove the pleats since they are soft and easy to cut.
5. Dip a sturdy knife into boiling water and wipe off the water with a dry cloth.
6. Divide and cut the separate layers into equal square portions.
7. Dip the knife into the water regularly since the heated blade will ensure a neat cut.
8. Serve with the filigree on top of the cake squares.

Shards and Christmas trees

1. Remove the Christmas trees from the cake and set them aside to be served with the cake squares.
2. Dip a sturdy knife into boiling water and wipe off the water with a dry cloth.
3. You can either remove the shards from the sides of the cake or cut through them.
4. Cut the cake into equal square portions.
5. Serve with Christmas trees on top of the squares.

Retro polka dot collar

1. Remove the truffles and chocolate spirals from the top of the cake and set aside to be served with the sliced cake.
2. Dip a sturdy knife into boiling water and wipe off the water with a dry cloth.
3. Leave the polka dot collar on the cake and cut the cake into equal portions.
4. Dip the knife into the water before you cut the collar, since the heated blade will make the cutting easier and the cake will be sliced neatly.
5. Serve with truffles and chocolate spirals on top of the slices.

Ice cream scoops

1. Remove a number of the ice cream curls from the bottom layer of cake and set these aside to be served with the cake squares.
2. The cake can be taken apart, layer by layer, as it was assembled – use an egg-lifter to separate and remove the top layers from the bottom one.
3. Remove the wooden skewers from the bottom layer.
4. Dip a sturdy knife into boiling water and wipe off the water with a dry cloth.
5. Cut the separate cake layers into equal square portions. The ice cream scoops are quite small and, if you try to cut between them, you will not have to remove all of scoops.
6. Dip the knife into the water regularly since the heated blade will ensure that the squares are cut neatly.
7. Serve the cake squares with ice cream curls on top of each piece.

Triangles

1. Dip a sturdy knife into boiling water and wipe off the water with a dry cloth.
2. You can either remove the triangles from the sides of the cake or cut through them.
3. Cut the cake into equal square portions.
4. Dip the knife into the water regularly since the heated blade will ensure that the squares are cut neatly.
5. Lift the squares carefully using a cake-lifter so as to prevent the berries and shavings from falling off.
6. Serve the cake with the remaining triangles, berries and shavings stacked on top of the squares.

Individual cakes

1. The cakes can be served as is. Alternatively, dip a sturdy knife into boiling water and wipe off the water with a dry cloth. Cut the individual cakes in half and serve one half per person.

Polka dot panels

1. Remove the chocolate daisies from the top of the cake and set them aside to be served with the sliced cake.
2. Dip a sturdy knife into boiling water and wipe off the water with a dry cloth.
3. Remove the panels from the sides of the cake or cut through them. Cut the cake into equal portions.
4. Dip the knife into the water before you cut the panels, since the heated blade will make it easier to cut through the chocolate and the cake will be sliced neatly.
5. Serve with the chocolate daisies and bits of the panels on top of the slices.

Candy-stripe curved collar

1. Remove the roses and leaves from the top of the cake and set them aside to be served with the sliced cake.
2. Dip a sturdy knife into boiling water and wipe off the water with a dry cloth.
3. Cut through the curved collar and the cake, dividing the cake into equal portions.
4. Dip the knife into the water before you cut the curved collar, since the heated blade will make it easy to cut through it and the cake will be sliced neatly.
5. Serve with the roses and leaves on top of the slices of cake.

Funky rolls and shavings

The cupcakes are not cut.

Square polka dot cake

1. Remove the chocolate dots on the toothpicks from the top layer and set them aside to be served with the cake squares.
2. Dip a sturdy knife into boiling water and wipe off the water with a dry cloth.
3. You can either remove the dots from the sides of the cake or cut through them.
4. Cut the cake into equal square portions.
5. Dip the knife into the water regularly since the heated blade will ensure that the squares are cut neatly.
6. Serve with the dots on top of the square pieces of cake.

Cigarillos and truffles

1. Remove the truffles from the layers of the cake and set them aside to be served with the sliced cake.
2. The cake can be taken apart, layer by layer, as it was assembled – use an egg-lifter to separate and remove the top layers from the bottom one.
3. You do not have to remove the cigarillos since you can easily fit a knife between them.
4. Remove the wooden sticks from the layers.
5. Dip a sturdy knife into boiling water and wipe off the water with a dry cloth.
6. Cut the separate cakes into equal portions.
7. Dip the knife into the water regularly since the heated blade will ensure a neat cut.
8. Serve the truffles with the slices of cake.

Full lace collar

1. The cake can be taken apart, layer by layer, as it was assembled – use an egg-lifter to separate and remove the top layers from the bottom one.
2. You do not have to remove the lace collar since it is easy to cut through it.
3. Remove the skewers from the layers.
4. Dip a sturdy knife into boiling water and wipe off the water with a dry cloth.
5. Cut the individual cakes into equal portions.
6. Dip the knife into the water before you cut the lace collar, since the heated blade will make it easier to cut through it and the cake will be sliced neatly.
7. Serve pieces of the lace collar with the cake.

Light and dark stripes

1. Remove the roses or berries from the layers of the cake and set them aside to be served with the sliced cake.
2. The cake can be taken apart, layer by layer, as it was assembled – use an egg-lifter to separate and remove the top layers from the bottom one.
3. Remove the wooden skewers from the bottom layer.
4. Remove the dark and light stripes from the sides of the cake or cut through them when you cut the cake.
5. Dip a sturdy knife into boiling water and wipe off the water with a dry cloth.

6. Cut the individual cakes into equal square portions.
7. Regularly dip the knife into the hot water since the heated blade makes it easier to cut the cake neatly.
8. Serve the cake squares with light and dark stripes and roses or berries.

Flaky shavings and lilies

1. Remove the arum lilies from the layers of the cake and set them aside to be served with the sliced cake.
2. The cake can be taken apart, layer by layer, as it was assembled – use an egg-lifter to separate and remove the top layer from the bottom one.
3. You do not have to remove the shavings since they are easy to cut.
4. Remove the wooden skewers from the bottom layer.
5. Dip a sturdy knife into boiling water and wipe off the water with a dry cloth.
6. Cut the individual cakes into equal portions.
7. Dip the knife into the water before you cut the shavings, since the heated blade will make it easier to cut through them and the cake will be sliced neatly.
8. Serve the arum lilies with the slices of cake.

Lace and collar

1. Remove the truffles and flowers from the layers of the cake and set them aside to be served with the slices of cake.
2. The cake can be taken apart, layer by layer, as it was assembled – use an egg-lifter to separate and remove the top layer from the bottom one.
3. You do not have to remove the lace and collar since they are easy to cut.
4. Remove the skewers from the bottom layer.
5. Dip a sturdy knife into boiling water and wipe off the water with a dry cloth.
6. Cut the individual cakes into equal portions.
7. Dip the knife into the water before you cut the lace and collar, since the heated blade will make it easier to cut through them and the cake will be sliced neatly.
8. Serve the slices with truffles and flowers.

Wrinkled layered collar

1. Remove the chocolate twirly whirlys and the chocolate initials from the layers of the cake and set these aside to be served with the slices of cake.
2. The cake can be taken apart, layer by layer, as it was assembled – use an egg-lifter to separate and remove the top layers from the bottom one.
3. You do not have to remove the wrinkled collars since they are easy to cut.
4. Remove the skewers from the layers of the cake.
5. Dip a sturdy knife into boiling water and wipe off the water with a dry cloth.
6. Cut the individual cakes into equal portions.
7. Dip the knife into the water before you cut the wrinkled collars, since the heated blade will make it easier to cut through them and the cake will be sliced neatly.
8. Serve the chocolate twirly whirlys with the slices of cake.

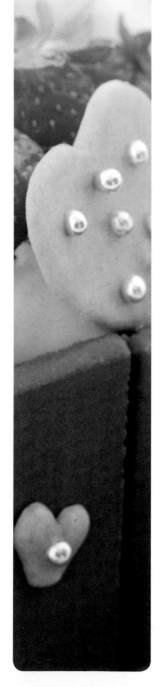

Storing cakes

1. The assembled cake can be kept in a cool, dark cupboard or in an airtight container for up to 3 days. If you think it is necessary, you can cover the cake with plastic cling wrap.
2. Do not expose the cake to direct sunlight, e.g. by leaving it close to a window, since the chocolate will melt.
3. Do not leave the assembled cake in the refrigerator since droplets of water will appear on the surface of the chocolate as a result of the humidity. This can cause ugly spots and streaks.
4. The sliced cake can be kept in an airtight container in the refrigerator for up to 5 days or in the deepfreeze for up to 3 months.
5. The assembled cake can be frozen for up to 3 months, should circumstances call for this. However, the entire cake must be covered securely in plastic cling wrap. When you wish to serve it, remove the cake from the deepfreeze and allow it to thaw in the refrigerator without removing the cling wrap. The droplets of water will appear on the plastic cover and not to the cake itself. Remove the cake, still covered cling wrap, from the refrigerator and leave it to reach room temperature before removing the cover. The chocolate may still develop white streaks because of the exposure to extreme temperatures.

Transporting cakes

1. If you wish to transport the cake to someone as a gift or if it was baked on order and has to be delivered to a client, place it in a sturdy box on non-slip fabric.
2. Place a non-slip mat under the box in the boot of your car.
3. Make sure that direct sunlight does not shine on the cake through the window since the chocolate may melt.
4. Turn on the air-conditioner to lower the temperature inside the car.
5. If you are delivering the cake to a restaurant or function venue, make sure that the cake is be placed in a cool area or in an air-conditioned room.
6. Always take along a few extra trimmings, some chocolate and a few Ziploc plastic bags, just in case trimmings fall or break off during transportation. You can use a Ziploc bag and quickly melt some chocolate in the microwave oven at the venue to repair any damage.

Templates

Dot flowers

Hearts

Christmas trees

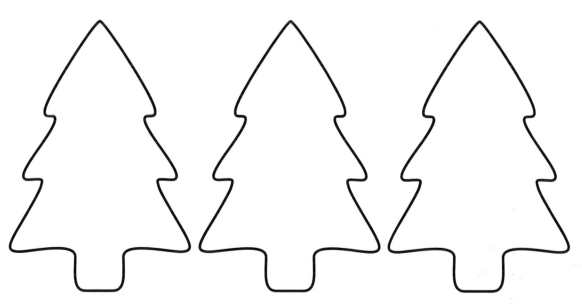

Daisies

Cupcake wrapper for standard-sized cupcakes

Your template must be 4.5 cm x 21 cm.

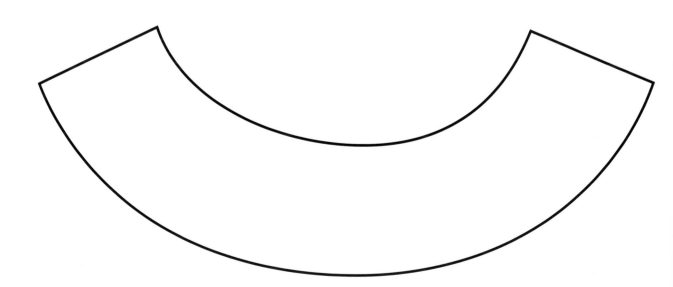

Suppliers

SOUTH-AFRICA

TAKE2
Imported tools, equipment, cutters
  and baking tins
Go to the USA or UK section:
home and kitchen
www.takealot.com

WANTITALL
Imported tools, equipment, cutters
  and baking supplies
www.wantitall.co.za

South Bakels
Baking supplies, Choccex cooking
  chocolate, cake boards
Cape Town Tel: 021-951 1388
Johannesburg Tel. 011- 673 2100
Nelspruit Tel: 013- 7523974
East-London Tel: 043- 7362941
Port-Elizabeth Tel: 041- 399 6600
Bloemfontein Tel: 051- 432 8445
www.sbakels.co.za

BAKER'S EMPORIUM
Baking supplies and choccex cooking
  chocolate
Tel: 021-949 0631

VALUE BAKING SUPPLIES
Baking supplies and cooking
chocolate, chocolate discs
Tel: 021-981 0304
www.valuesupplies.co.za

THE BAKING TIN
Baking supplies and Orley cooking
  chocolate
Cape Town and agents around the
country Tel: 021-704 1710
www.thebakingtin.co.za

CAB FOODS
Baking supplies, Orley chocolate,
chocolate discs
Tel: 021-981 6778
sales@cabfoods.co.za

THE CHOCOLATE DEN
Baking supplies and chocolate
  products
Tel: 011-453 8160
www.chocolateden.co.za

KOCO TRADING
Belgian couverture and coating/
  compound chocolate, truffles
  and cigarillos
Tel: 021-949 4410
www.kocotrading.co.za

CHOCOLATES BY TOMES
African origin couverture chocolate,
  chocolate discs, chocolate sticks
  and truffles
Tel: 021-905 7214
lorraine@tomeschocolates.co.za

USA

WILTON
Baking equipment and candy coating
www.wilton.com

Make 'n Mold
Candy coating
www.makenmold.com

Cake Art
Candy coating
www.cakeart.com

UK

Squires-Shop
Baking supplies, chocolate coating
  and Belgian chocolate
www.squires-shop.com

Barry Callebaut
Cocoa, chocolate and confectionary
  products
www.barry-callebaut.com

Jane Asher Party Cakes
Baking equipment
www.jane-asher.co.uk

Notes